MOMENTS
OF
GRACE AND BEAUTY

Forty Stories of Kindness, Courage, and Generosity in a Troubled World

Roland Merullo

MOMENTS OF GRACE AND BEAUTY
Forty Stories of Kindness, Courage,
and Generosity in a Troubled World

PFP INC
publisher@pfppublishing.com
PO Box 829
Byfield, MA 01922

May 2019
Printed in the United States of America

ISBN-13: 978-1-7324322-3-9

Front Cover Photo
© Amanda S. Merullo

(also available in eBook and hardcover formats)

Other Books by Roland Merullo

Fiction

Leaving Losapas
A Russian Requiem
Revere Beach Boulevard
In Revere, In Those Days
A Little Love Story
Golfing with God
Breakfast with Buddha
American Savior
Fidel's Last Days
The Talk-Funny Girl
Lunch with Buddha
Vatican Waltz
The Return
Dinner with Buddha
Rinpoche's Remarkable Ten-Week Weight Loss Clinic
The Delight of Being Ordinary
Once Night Falls

Non Fiction

Passion for Golf: In Pursuit of the Innermost Game

Revere Beach Elegy: A Memoir of Home & Beyond

*The Italian Summer: Golf, Food,
and Family at Lake Como*

*Demons of the Blank Page: 15 Obstacles That Keep You
From Writing & How To Conquer Them*

Taking the Kids to Italy

*The Ten Commandments of Golf Etiquette: How to Make
the Game More Enjoyable for Yourself
and for Everyone Else on the Course*

For Amanda

Introduction

When our daughters were young, whenever they'd see or hear about someone behaving badly, I'd say to them: That's a lesson in how not to be. These stories—examples of generous or brave moments or people I've seen or known in my own life—are the opposite.

The world seems to be overflowing with trouble. In so many places authoritarian rulers flourish while the pillars of democracy and decency crack. Facts struggle to compete with bizarre conspiracy theories and blatant lies supported by sophisticated propaganda. We have school shootings, high rates of addiction, suicide, and depression, and consciously or otherwise most of us worry about climate change and what it will mean for us, our kids, and grandkids.

Those are the things that make the headlines and dominate the TV news. But every day around the world there are also billions of acts of kindness, courage, generosity, and grace, and we don't hear much about them.

This past December, at the start of another gray, cold, New England winter, I decided to make a list of some of the remarkable acts I've witnessed, the generous, kind, and brave people I've known. The idea was to post the stories on my Facebook page, one every day for the last month of a turbulent year. I did that, and the response was so enthusiastic that I decided I'd expand the list and make it into a small book.

It's much easier to write about the evil in the world than about the good. Writers who focus on violence, greed, ugliness, and hypocrisy can seem more sophisticated, more intelligent, more mature, more aware of the world's true nature. I see the troubles as clearly as anyone, but I think they get more than their share of coverage. That cargo of bad news can act as a weight on the human mind.

I put together this small book as a counterweight.

Nothing that was worthy in the past departs; no truth or goodness realized by man ever dies.

Thomas Carlyle

~1~

In the fall of 1986, my wife Amanda took a leave from her job as a photographer at the Clark Art Institute in Williamstown, Massachusetts, I sold my blue Dodge pickup, emptied my bank account—$1,200—and we went to live in Mexico for three months. We were childless then and in our early thirties and, though we knew we'd come home with empty pockets, we thought the Mexico trip would be a nice, inexpensive adventure. There were other reasons, too. I was hoping I could avoid back surgery for a ruptured disc by staying away from my one-man carpentry business for a while. And I was also hoping I could use the time to finish the first draft of a first novel I'd been working on for several years.

We spent a month each in extremely modest hotels in Merida, San Luis Potosi, and Mazatlan, living simply, spending $15 a day, total, for food and lodging. We'd go out together for breakfast and then, for the first part of the day, I'd stay in the hotel room and write; Amanda—who speaks Spanish well—would wander the city taking photos. I wound up having back surgery a month after we returned home—so much for that hope—but I did finish a good draft of my novel, which, five long years later, was published by Houghton Mifflin as *Leaving Losapas.* Amanda came home with a lot of great photographs.

The moment I want to describe occurred one October morning in San Luis Potosi, an old colonial city in central Mexico, 250 miles north of Mexico City. There was a restaurant near the city's central park where Amanda and I would often have breakfast. We were sitting there, finishing our *caffe con leche* and *huevos rancheros,* when a middle-aged Mexican man in an expensive gray suit and white dress shirt came in and sat not far from us. A few minutes later a young boy stepped through the door, barefoot, dressed in rags, and started to go from customer to customer, begging for coins.

Before the boy could reach our table, the owner of the place chased him out. Just then, the man in the gray suit was served his eggs, meat, and toast. He immediately made them into a breakfast sandwich, wrapped the sandwich in a napkin, then got up from his table and hurried out into the city, chasing after the beggar boy to give him his breakfast.

~ 2 ~

One March, when our two daughters were young and we were all anxious to escape the end of the New England winter, my mother accompanied us to South Carolina on their spring school vacation. We rented a condo at a gated golf community called Pawleys Plantation, at the southernmost end of the Myrtle Beach strip, and we took turns playing golf, watching cooking shows on TV, having fun with the girls, and sampling local eating places.

Ma was a devout Catholic and asked if we could take her to mass on Sunday. We did a little online research and found a Catholic church in Georgetown, a steel mill city half an hour to the south. At the appointed hour on Sunday morning we put on our best clothes and drove down SC 17 to Georgetown, only to discover that there had been a mix-up. Either the church's website had it wrong, or their phone message had it wrong, or we'd misunderstood: we arrived 45 minutes late, just as the front doors were opening and people were streaming out.

"Sorry, Mum," I said. "Want to try another

church?"

She was up for it, as she was up for so many of the things we did on our travels around the United States and abroad with her. My mother was a giving, resilient woman who had been through a lot in her long life: health troubles, loss of her beloved sister and best friend when she was 21, sudden loss of her husband when he was 66. Toughened by those experiences, and by living through the Great Depression and serving in World War II, she was always ready to help out with the kids, never a complaint no matter what the circumstances. Traveling with us in Rome when she was 78, she slept on a pull-out bed for a month. In South Carolina, though I think it was a first, she let us take her to a Protestant church.

The first church we came upon was a pretty, red brick place with a square bell tower, the Bethel A.M.E. Their service started at 11:00 so we were just in time. When we climbed the front steps and went through the door, we realized we were the only white people in the building. We're respectful types, we were dressed nicely. I decided to assume that if we acted appropriately we'd be welcome, but I had no idea what kind of welcome we'd receive.

It seemed to me that, although the pastor was a man, women ran the church. Near the entrance and scattered around the nave were extremely well dressed, mostly elderly women. Two of them approached us right away, handed us programs, and welcomed us so sincerely and so warmly that any worry about being out of place immediately disappeared. We filed into the back pew and were then treated to what Amanda later said was the most spiritually elevating service she'd ever attended. Two hours of singing and prayer, with a lengthy, moving sermon on feeling good about yourself, feeling beloved by God, no matter what you did for a living, no matter what your status in the world.

Several times the people in the pew in front of us turned around to help us understand what to do at a particular moment in the unfamiliar service, and at one point the pastor asked visitors to stand. We already felt conspicuous, but, along with one other visitor, we stood and said where we were from and were applauded and welcomed again.

What I especially liked about the service was that the pastor called everyone to communion—everyone, no matter their perceived state of grace—and that the sign of peace went on and on, with men, women, and children walking around the church shaking hands and embracing, not simply greeting those in the nearest pews. I was proud, too, of our girls, who were small then, and fidgety, but who sat through the long service mostly without complaint.

The men and women in that building had every reason to treat us differently than they did. Though we aren't the descendants of slave-owning families, we were staying and playing golf at a former rice plantation that had been worked, no doubt, by the enslaved ancestors of some of the people in those pews. But we didn't feel the slightest tinge of hostility. Just the opposite in fact. We were seen as the respectful people we are, humble enough to think that maybe the human mind wasn't the apex of intelligence in the universe, that maybe we should give thanks for being alive, maybe we should allow for the possibility of some larger spirit, or at least take an hour out of the week to do something other than work, play golf, or worry about bills.

I thought of that gracious welcome when, some years later, a different group of A.M.E. worshippers, a little farther down SC 17, extended a similar welcome to a white man. . .who then turned a gun on them and slaughtered nine of his hosts. I think of them just about every time I hear of another racially charged incident in this country. But mostly I just think of them, as I used to tell the girls, as people who offered us a lesson in how to be on this earth.

~ 3 ~

My cousin Lois Ann Holbrook is about my own age and, despite the fact that she lives 1,000 miles away, we've been close since childhood. After graduating from college in her home state of Indiana, Lois met and married a wonderful man named Dan Holbrook. They had a close, loving relationship and were enjoying life with their two young kids, Hilary and James, when Dan went into the hospital for what should have been a routine operation. He survived the operation but something went wrong in the recovery room, the kind of thing that happens one time in a million recoveries, and he died in a matter of minutes.

I flew out for the funeral and I remember the sadness of it, Lois and her family encased in grief and shock, her young children perplexed beyond any describing.

Twenty-some years have passed. While she had a lot of help and emotional support from her mother, sisters, friends, and brothers-in-law, Lois raised those kids on her own, on a teacher's salary.

I never heard a whisper of complaint or bitterness from her, and the young woman and young man she raised are two of the kindest, warmest, and most creative souls on the planet.

Sometimes heroism is like that, measured not in grand acts, but in a million mundane sacrifices, years of invisible effort that bear magnificent fruit. You can see it everywhere: good people—parents especially, but aunts, uncles, grandparents, teachers, nurses, therapists—making someone else's life better, quietly, steadily, without fuss. When I wrote Lois to ask permission to post something about her in my Facebook series on brave people, she wrote back saying I was welcome to do that, but "You know I don't see my story as special or admirable."

I do.

~ 4 ~

Sometimes heroism takes a more obvious form.

Not long ago we noted the 77th anniversary of the attack on Pearl Harbor, so, since these appreciations are about people who have inspired me, I thought I'd mention two brave cousins of mine who served in Vietnam.

Jim Haydock was in the army infantry in Nha Trang, lugging a twenty-three-pound radio around in 110-degree heat through a jungle thick with Viet Cong. Cleaning out our attic recently I came across a letter he sent me when I was 13. He avoided the harsh details and wrote, instead, a matter-of-fact account of his days, wondering how he'd fare if he made it home to the Massachusetts winters after acclimating to Southeast Asia. Like so many veterans, he doesn't talk much about the war, but no doubt he called in air support while under fire, and also managed evacuations for his wounded comrades. And no doubt he lived with fear night and day.

John Aucella, son of a WWII Flying Tigers pilot, volunteered for the Marines when most people I knew were doing everything they possibly could to avoid being drafted. He was trained at the flight school in Pensacola, Florida and ended up flying medevac helicopters out of DaNang at about the same time Jim was serving.

Twice shot down, John earned the Bronze Star and Distinguished Flying Cross. For a while during the first summer after his return to our hometown, John and I got up early and raced ten speed bikes along Revere Beach Boulevard. Like Jim, he never said much about the war. But some twenty-five years later, sitting next to me at a family wedding, he told me that, by the end of his time in Vietnam, as soon as he was told to go out on a mission, he'd start to shake uncontrollably. He'd board the helicopter, let someone else fly it to the zone of combat, and then he'd take over the controls. In the heat of battle, the shaking disappeared. He'd land the helicopter, sit there, a perfect target, while the wounded were brought aboard, and then he'd lift off and head back over the trees. At which point the shaking would start again and someone else would take over.

I mentioned John's time as a Medevac pilot to a friend who'd served in the same war. The friend's comment: "Those guys had balls of steel."

Both men fought some battles after returning home, and how could they not? The human brain isn't made to go from the horrors of war to the domestic scene. I've often wondered how they survived, psychologically, immersed in a world where we fret over what kind of topping to put on an ice cream sundae, after they'd spent a year worrying about being shot to death, or seeing friends wounded, maimed, or killed. John died a few years ago of kidney failure. Like so many of the Vietnam vets I know, Jim now battles cancer. He has the companionship of his loving kids and supportive wife, Alice, just as John had the support of a loving family.

There's a lot of flag-waving these days, a lot of lip service about our heroes in uniform. As a combat veteran friend of mine once told me, all the men and women who served in Vietnam weren't heroic. True enough. But, like other veterans, so many of them lived with a kind of physical and psychological vulnerability and exposure to terror that even those of us with the best imaginations can't grasp.

~ 5 ~

This past April I was invited to Little Rock, Arkansas, to talk about a novel of mine, *Breakfast with Buddha,* to members of an open-minded Episcopal church, St. Mark's. I arrived on the previous night and stayed at a nearby hotel. On the day of the presentation I asked the hotel clerk where I might go for lunch, and she said there was a mall that had a few good restaurants in it. "But it's a mile away so you might want to call a cab."

I told her I enjoyed walking and I set out to follow her directions. It wasn't the most scenic route—uphill along a road that had two busy lanes in each direction. But at the mall I found a good Mediterranean cafe and enjoyed a lamb kebab plate with hummus and rice, a favorite dish of mine. The portions were large and I took away part of the kebab in a container, thinking I might give it to a young man I'd seen asking for handouts on the street corner.

The young man had disappeared. I retraced my route—using the other side of the busy road—and, ahead of me, saw a different man standing on a different corner, cardboard sign in hand. I decided to offer him the take-out food, but when I looked up again I saw that he'd stepped out into the line of cars stopped at the light and was standing behind a large blue SUV there. I wondered if there was some kind of altercation going on, or if the man had taken leave of his senses and was blocking traffic in one of the lanes.

I was close to his corner when the light changed and I realized that the SUV was stalled at the bottom of the highway off-ramp, a worried-looking woman at the wheel, cars lining up behind her, and that the man on the corner was trying to push the huge vehicle forward by himself. I trotted over and took up a position next to him. Behind us, a young guy in a pickup pulled to the curb and jumped out and the three of us were able to push the woman's SUV, very slowly, across four lanes of traffic and into the hotel parking lot. No one in four lines of blocked cars so much as tooted the horn.

I offered the take-out food, and the man who'd been standing on the corner accepted it, showing a smile. "Kebab?" he said. "I love kebab!" The woman thanked all of us. It was a tiny good deed, but it occurred to me afterwards that the three of us with our hands on the back of the SUV might have represented three different factions of American society—an African American man, a white guy who seemed like a good ol' southerner in his pickup, and one of those elite Northeast liberals who cause so much trouble in the world.

We shook hands, nodded to each other, went our separate ways. A tiny good deed. No risk, a little effort, nothing worthy of the evening news. But, against the background of a divided nation, there was a sense of camaraderie and simple decency in that moment, as if we were human beings first, and other labels fell to second or third place.

~ 6 ~

For several years when the girls were young and we weren't bound by their school schedules, I taught in the Writers In Paradise conference in St. Petersburg, Florida. The conference was organized by my friends Sterling Watson and Dennis Lchane and I was honored to be part of it. In addition to teaching daily workshops, our duties included giving one public reading to students and faculty and any local people who cared to stop in and listen.

It was my night to read, and Amanda and the girls and I had gone out to dinner with old college friends Rich and Sue Clarendon, who'd been kind enough to drive up from their home in Bradenton. We'd finished the meal and had stepped out into the warm Florida darkness when I heard someone yell, "He went flying through the air!" It was a strange cry, delivered in a frightened voice—almost a scream—and a second later I realized that a man had been hit by a car and was lying in the middle of the busy street.

I called 911, gave them the location of the accident, and then hurried over to the injured man. He was lying in a pool of his own blood. Two young women were kneeling on the pavement beside him, holding him and speaking to him. Another minute and there were police and ambulance lights flashing against the buildings and the first responders arrived.

There was nothing to do but leave them and go give my reading to several hundred people at the auditorium at Eckerd College. In the paper the next day I read that the man had been killed: for unspecified reasons he'd stepped right out into traffic on the dark street. I thought about the two women there, strangers it had seemed, passersby, kneeling on the bloody pavement and comforting him in his last moments.

~ 7 ~

We live on a winding two-lane road that runs through a high valley in the western part of Massachusetts. The hills to either side of the road are covered with mixed hardwoods and some spruce and pine, and cut by streams that funnel into a small river that travels just beside the guardrails in places.

There's not much traffic on this road except for the hours, morning and afternoon, when people are leaving for work or returning home. In places there are stretches as long as half a mile where it's just woods, no driveways, no homes, nothing but the New England forest. We've seen all kinds of wildlife on our road—deer, coyote, black bear, fox, turkey, porcupine, possum, skunk, raccoon, great blue heron, a bald eagle, owls, hawks, pileated woodpeckers, snakes, lizards, moles, voles, even a black mink carrying her three babies across by the nape of the neck, one by one.

I walk a couple of miles on the road almost every day, and in warm weather it's a popular route for bicyclists and motorcyclists. Most of the drivers are courteous, and swing wide to give plenty of room for those traveling on foot or bike. But there are also those who use the less peopled sections as their own personal garbage dump, tossing beer cans, take-out boxes, shot bottles, diapers, magazines, and assorted other junk out the window when they think no one is watching.

Our closest neighbors, Art and Pat Spencer, are wonderful people. They'll help out with snow shoveling, watch the house when we're gone, bring over gifts on birthdays and anniversaries, and generally set a high standard for the human race.

Art's a retired navy vet and another regular roadside walker. Half the time he'll take a plastic bag along with him and return from his walk with a load of other people's refuse. No big fuss. No complaint or criticism. He doesn't do it to earn the five cent return fee on recyclables—a lot of what he picks up isn't recyclable at all. He does it because he has a sense of civic duty—to use an old fashioned term he'd probably never use. It's not his garbage. He just cleans it off the roadside for the sake of the other people who walk and ride there, to make it safer for those on two wheels, and more pleasant for the rest of us.

~ 8 ~

During my second tour with USIA cultural exhibits in the former USSR (May, 1987-June, 1988) my title was General Services Officer and my duties included supervising setup and takedown in each city, clearing exhibit displays and supplies through customs, driving the forklift and the exhibit car, and working with the local police to keep the large crowds (up to 15,000 visitors a day) under control.

I loved that job, loved the variety of it, loved spending the days with Soviet laborers and policemen (though the customs officials could be pains in the *zhopa*). In addition to the policemen, there were always plainclothes security people on duty, stationed throughout the 10,000 square foot exhibition. Some of them were friendlier than others, but my guess is they all kept their eyes open and reported to the KGB.

That spring we spent two months in Tashkent—it's the capital of the independent nation of Uzbekistan now, but in those days it was part of the Soviet Union. One of the security guys there was a tough looking character—strong build, thinning reddish-blond hair, cauliflower ears, a manner just this side of gruff. I'll call him Anton, but I don't remember his name. Clearly he'd been boxer in his youth, but by then, early forties, his boxing career was finished and he was picking up temporary work on the American exhibit, earning a few rubles a day. I used to look at him and think: he's part of the viciousness of this country, one of the guys paid to beat up dissidents and frighten ordinary people away. Maybe even a torturer.

Sometimes our jobs overlapped: he'd give me a message about crowd control issues, or I'd relay something to him from our director. Every once in a while we'd fall into a brief conversation. Benign subjects like weather, family, sports. I neither liked nor disliked him; he looked and acted like a tough guy, an enforcer, and I had my preconceived notions, but I never saw him push or try to intimidate anyone, and his speech was quiet, his manner reserved.

Late in our time in Tashkent, Anton came up to me on the exhibit property, out of earshot of his fellow workers, and asked if Amanda and I would be willing to come to his home for dinner. I was completely surprised and more than slightly wary. We were allowed to accept such invitations (they were frequent) as long as we were accompanied by another American, so, not wanting to cause offence, I said sure, we'd be happy to come. We set a date and Anton gave me directions.

On the night of the dinner, Amanda and I bought something to give as a housewarming gift—flowers, maybe, or some American souvenir, I don't recall—and made the very long trolley ride out to the far edge of the city. Anton met us at the stop so we wouldn't get lost, and led us on a ten-minute walk through a hideous Soviet housing development, one ugly, poorly built, ten-story concrete apartment building after the next, the corners crooked, the entrances littered, the metal doors squeaking and dented, the benches broken. We followed him through a puddled courtyard, through a dark entrance, and up two flights of chipped concrete stairs.

It turned out that Anton and his wife lived in a tiny two-room apartment with a bathroom barely large enough for a toilet and its user. After a few minutes, we learned that Anton's wife's mother lived there with them—three people in two rooms, not exactly the kind of accommodation reserved for KGB spies or torturers. She had gone to see a friend in order to give us more space. There was no dining room, so our hosts set a piece of plywood out on their white bedspread and served the meal there. Anton's wife was garishly made up, with raccoon eye mascara, as if she'd imagined that was how women looked in our world on special occasions. I don't imagine they'd ever had—or ever again would have—American guests, and Amanda and I were complimentary and kind.

The food—which likely cost them a week's pay and hours in line—was perfectly good, and the hospitality warm, unaffected, and sincere. There was no sense of any political intrigue, no political discussion at all, just two couples with very different lives sharing a meal and a little conversation. Afterwards, Anton walked us back through the grim Soviet night to the trolley stop, and waited with us until we were safely aboard.

It was, for me, another lesson in being careful about judgment. For the rest of our days in that city, I never looked at Anton in the same way.

~ 9 ~

In 1996 I wrote a 20-part series of Op-Ed pieces for the *Philadelphia Inquirer* on the presidential primaries and election. Mike Leary, my editor, gave me all kinds of interesting assignments connected to the campaigns. I went to the conventions, to the two big and very political St. Patrick's Day parades in Chicago, and anywhere else that seemed linked to the issues of the day.

My favorite of those assignments lasted four days and produced several columns. I flew to Little Rock, rented a car, and drove in a big loop, through Bob Dole's hometown—Russell, Kansas; to Ross Perot's hometown—Texarkana, Texas; to Bill Clinton's hometown—Hope, Arkansas; and then back to Little Rock. For the most part I stayed on back roads and visited small towns. I'd approach people on the street and ask them to tell me the first word that came to mind when I said "Dole" and "Clinton" and "Perot".

Responses ranged from "Monster", "Anti-Christ", and "Non-human", to "Decent", "Fool", "Hero", "Christian", and "Ears," and there were some funny moments having to do with my Boston accent. At one point I approached two women on a sidewalk in Oklahoma and said, "I'm with the *Philadelphia Inquirer* and I'm writing an article on the presidential elections," and one woman turned to the other and said, "I can't understand a word he's sayin'!"

North Central Kansas surprised me. I'd expected the whole state to be flat as an ironing board, but the landscape around Dole's hometown was a fascinating quilt of small gullies and rises, plateaus and streambeds. I went out for a drive there, wandering along the back roads through farmland and prairie, and soon became lost—a specialty of mine. These were pre-GPS days, but it didn't worry me. It was mid-afternoon and I knew I'd get back to the town at some point. As I was going along a gravel road I saw an old blue pickup coming the other way. I stopped and waved a hand, and the driver, a man close to sixty, pulled up beside me.

I explained the situation. He laughed and told me I was only a mile or so from town, and we fell into conversation. After about three minutes he said, "You like bar-be-que?" I had a little trouble with *his* accent and asked him to repeat the question. He did. I said, yes, I liked barbecue fine. "How about coming to our house for dinner then? My wife fixes a good bar-be-que."

I told him I'd be happy to. He gave me the address and directions, and that evening, after I'd done a bit of writing in the hotel room, I headed over to his place. He and his wife lived in a modest ranch house on an ordinary street at the edge of town. Their idea of barbecue—maybe it's the Kansas definition—turned out to be steaks grilled outdoors, no fancy sauces. They put together a tasty meal and we sat around in their home and talked for an hour and a half.

At the end of the visit, the man presented me with a piece of sandstone about eight inches tall, shaped like a thick cigar tube but square and with sharp edges. *DOLE 96* was cut into the stone, but there was no sense he was campaigning or trying to influence my vote; it was simply a gesture, a gift, a token. The man and his wife knew my politics, and I knew theirs—we had talked about that over dinner—but not for a second did our differences have any bearing on the congeniality of the meal. I don't remember their names. They were simple people, not very educated judging by their speech, but gracious and generous and so optimistic about humanity that they'd invited a total stranger into their home, fed him, and handed him a small gift, without any ulterior motives whatsoever.

To this day I display that memento conspicuously on the bookshelf in the room where I write. It reminds me of a more civil way of discussing politics, and of ordinary human kindness.

~ 10 ~

A tribute to aunts.

I grew up with twelve aunts, a pantheon of re-markable women, world-class givers of love. Among them were several great cooks, and several people you'd call up in a certain mood just to be reminded, by the affection in their voice, that things would eventually work out; women who raised their daughters to be strong and to feel good about themselves; some big Red Sox fans; some politically outspoken, some politically neu-tral; some deeply religious and some not. One of them pushed her daughter out of the way before being hit by a careening car driven by a drunk driver, saving the young girl from injury but con-demning herself to a life of pain and limping. One of them raised four kids while battling rheumatoid arthritis. One of them, a nurse, cared for her par-ents and two of her sisters in their final months. One of them was a loving and incredibly patient companion to a husband with Alzheimer's; one of them suffered from Alzheimer's at the end of her life. Two of them inspired Amanda and me with their world travels and penchant for truth-telling.

A bunch of them served as role models for us in the raising of our daughters. One of them—who would have been my thirteenth—died of tuberculosis when she was in her twenties, long before I was born.

Without exception, the twelve I knew were the kind of people who'd welcome you into their home—sometimes on no or short notice—and offer you a cup of tea or a meal, listen to your stories, ask about your schoolwork or, later, your children. Though several of them had lives peppered with various kinds of troubles—medical, financial, marital—they were part of a tough generation, and there wasn't much complaint.

Without exception, those who were married (one was not) outlived their husbands, and experienced—or are still experiencing—a long stretch of lonely years.

My mother's sister, Marian, had the worst luck in that department. She lost her husband Walter to heart disease when they were in their thirties and had three young kids. Marian raised them in a housing project, supporting them by working as a secretary in a law office. Though she'd never gone to college, her great passion in life was her love of books, and she was a lifelong supporter of the local library.

I didn't tell her I was trying to publish a novel; I told almost no one in my twelve years of unofficial 'apprenticeship'. On the day my first book was accepted, June 29, 1989, I left the Houghton Mifflin offices in downtown Boston and floated around the city for an hour in a high no opiate could ever match. I took the subway to my hometown of Revere, bought a bottle of champagne at a liquor store on Broadway, walked the half mile west to my mother's house (she, too, had lost her husband), and surprised her with the news.

My mother wasn't much of a drinker—in fact, she liked to boast that she had never tasted so much as one sip of beer in her life—but when I lifted the champagne bottle out of its paper bag she placed two glasses on the table without hesitation. Literally, just as I was popping the cork, the doorbell rang. It was Aunt Marian. She happened to be driving past and thought she'd stop in and chat with her sister. She had no idea, at first, what the celebration was about, but when I told her the news, she was overjoyed. Another semi-teetotaler, she accepted a glass of champagne, and the three of us stood there in my mother's small kitchen and drank a grateful toast.

I remember the pleasure Aunt Marian took in that moment, echo of my own, and the pink glow on her cheeks after she'd emptied the glass. A bit of happiness for her—a book lover and supportive aunt—and a woman who lived a difficult life with dignity.

~ 11 ~

My father was a state office worker for most of his adult life—Director of the Industrial Accident Board—but he'd also spent some time at the Massachusetts State House as Personnel Secretary to centrist Republican governors Christian Herter and John Volpe. In that position he'd done a lot of favors for friends and relatives, and in later years, calling on that bank account of generosity, he was able to get me—and a number of my cousins—unusual and often unusually well-paying summer jobs. I sold Coke and popcorn at Fenway Park for a couple of years, collected tolls in the East Boston tunnels, drew a paycheck for not doing much in the Somerville District Court.

The most interesting, but not exactly the easiest of those jobs was working in a trailer at the base of the John Hancock Tower, when the 60-story building—still Boston's tallest—was under construction. I ran errands, put the ironworkers' checks in envelopes, made copies, and was bored to tears much of the time. But most afternoons one of the two main engineers on the job would come into the trailer and ask me to accompany him 'upstairs'. We'd ride up 50 or 55 floors in a shaky construction elevator and I'd follow him on his rounds, sometimes holding a six-foot surveyor's pole so he could check the cantilevers and floor levels.

I never walked on beams, but I was terrified most of the time anyway. The building swayed in the wind—as it was designed to do—and since there were no walls at that height, there would often be strong winds whipping across the open concrete floors.

One of the engineers—I'll call him Noel, but that wasn't his name—had a drinking problem, as did many of the ironworkers. He had other problems, too, and would often regale me with tales of his exploits in the Combat Zone bars after work. I was a naive 17-year-old, about to start my first year of college, and I listened to the stories with a mix of intimidation and curiosity, did what I was told on the job, and tried to deal with the fear in my belly every time Noel or the other engineer said, "Hey Kid, let's go upstairs."

For whatever reason, Noel did most of the surveying of the cantilevered corners, making sure the iron beams had been riveted into place correctly and they weren't drooping or lifting up above the level of the rest of the floor. Our work was in the mid-fifties by then, summer of 1971.

Along the outer edge of each floor a single safety cable had been strung at waist-height. On Noel's direction, I'd step over to the cable, turn my back to the 700 foot drop a yard or so on the other side of it, hold the marked rod as straight and still as I could, and let him 'shoot' it through the surveyor's transit and take a reading.

This was frightening enough, but one day he asked me to help him get a shot of a cantilever that extended out in a triangular shape on the other side of the cable. It would have meant stepping over the cable and out onto the windswept corner, nothing between me and a spectacular death but a few feet of flooring. He gave me the assignment this way—"Go on out there, would you, Kid?" I looked out at the cantilever, looked back and him and said, "Do you want me to?"

He got the message. Without making any fuss about it or even asking me a second time, toothless old drunken Noel waved me over to the transit and showed me how to focus the lens and take the reading. Then he took the rod himself and stepped out over the cable and stood there, calm as a monk in prayer, while I focused and gave him the number.

~ 12 ~

When she graduated from Phillips Exeter, our older daughter, Alexandra—Zanny, everyone calls her—decided she didn't want to go to college. She traveled for a bit, did some volunteer work in Naples, Italy, walked the 500-mile Camino de Santiago pilgrimage in Spain, then came home and found a job at The Hangar, a sports bar near UMass Amherst, so she could save for more travel. The Hangar was—and is—a friendly place, with pinball and pool tables, eight or ten TVs, and a simple menu that features wings, ribs, and salads.

Like most places that serve alcohol, however, there would be the occasional difficult client. The owner had hired a couple of imposing bouncer/waiters, Andy and Paul, guys who would look right at home on a Division I football team's offensive line. Trouble was rare, but this duo took care of obnoxious customers with panache and efficiency and just the right amount of force.

Zanny worked most nights until 1 a.m. or later and then went out into the large parking lot, found her car, and made the half-hour drive home. She's mature and well traveled, toughened by years of dealing with cystic fibrosis, and she's capable of taking care of herself, but, still, she was a young woman alone late at night in a dark place. At closing time, either Andy or Paul, or sometimes both Andy and Paul would step out the front door and make sure she reached her car without incident.

A gesture of friendship and decency, not part of their job description, that eased one father's mind.

~ 13 ~

At Phillips Exeter Academy in New Hampshire, I was in a senior-year writing class with a girl who grew into the well known novelist and memoirist Joyce Maynard. We've remained friends to this day. Early last year she wrote and asked if we could speak by phone, she had a project she thought I might be interested in.

The project turned out to be ghostwriting the life story of a remarkable woman named Pat McFarlane. I was, in fact, interested. I'd just finished a novel, so the timing was good. Pat and I spoke a couple of times by phone and exchanged notes by email. We discovered that we had a lot in common and a good line of communication, and in April we decided to start the project.

Pat grew up in the working class neighborhood of Roxborough, a section of Philadelphia and was the daughter of a man and woman who had not finished high school. She and her three brothers and parents shared a two-bedroom row house and, as kids often did in those days, spent a lot of time on the street corners and stoops playing with friends and neighbors.

Her parents sent her to Catholic school, where she excelled academically but often ran afoul of the nuns due to her gift of gab and love of socializing . . . in class. "In our neighborhood," she told me, "boys went to Vietnam after high school and girls went to work." But she earned a college degree, part-time, married, and she and her husband started working as house parents in group homes—for deaf men, for cognitively challenged adults, for teenage girls whose biological parents were incapable of raising them.

After years of that work, when her own fourth child went off kindergarten, Pat had a strong urge to start a business. She spent the better part of a year talking to friends, making lists, wondering what kind of business she was best suited for, hoping for something that would both put good into the world and allow her to spend a lot of time with her kids. She knew that she liked to travel, liked people, was good at organizing, and had often worked with the disabled (to use a word she dislikes).

She came up with the idea of taking mentally handicapped people on trips. She started small, escorting a handful of clients on one day-trip a month (to the Jersey shore, Phillies games, Amish country) and making one longer trip, as well, (Disneyworld, Hawaii, a cruise to Maine).

Little by little, year by year, with the support of husband Tom, she expanded the business—Special Vacations, it's called—and now, 27 years later, she runs 75 trips annually to places like Ireland and Bermuda and Las Vegas, sometimes taking as many as 120 people at a time.

In the course of writing the book, I went on several of these trips with her. It was an experience almost impossible to describe. Pat has assembled a staff of angels, most of them inner city Philadelphians, the most patient, loving, kind, and funny people I've ever had the pleasure of spending time with. Clients and employees alike treat her as a blend of mother, friend, boss, and blond, tough-talking god. In her late sixties now, she is indefatigable, unfailingly positive, even amidst the stresses of watching over a hundred travelers— some of whom are in wheelchairs, or can't feed themselves, or dress themselves, or speak, or hear, or see. All of whom exhibit a greater or lesser degree of what used to be called mental retardation (another term she studiously avoids).

On one of her trips, we went to an Amish home near Lancaster, Pennsylvania. There, without benefit of electricity, the family prepared a four-course meal for thirty visitors, and served us with a generous simplicity and straightforwardness that could serve as a spiritual primer. The Amish,

Pat's incredible staff, the happy, grateful travelers, and the woman herself—trying to do justice to all of them was a challenge I knew I would never quite meet.

The whole six-month project was an exercise in gratitude and humility for me. Pat and her staff made it onto my list of heroes, opening the world to tens of thousands of people who carry a heavy burden through this life, and who would normally have only the rarest opportunity to leave their homes.

~ 14 ~

When I was a boy, I had the good fortune of spending a lot of time around all four of my grandparents. My mother's parents, James and Catherine, lived a fifteen-minute walk from us. My father's parents, Joseph and Eleonora, lived downstairs until I was seven, and then we moved next door. Each of them handed down to me something precious.

My mother's mother was born in London and spoke clearly and beautifully with just a touch of the Old World in her words. She suffered terribly from rheumatoid arthritis, even becoming immune to painkillers late in her life. I appreciate her courage now, with my own, less serious arthritis struggles. I remember her gnarled hands, but my strongest memories are listening to her recite long poems by heart as she sat in a wheelchair in her kitchen on Olive Street. Sometimes when I write I can hear the rhythm of her speech.

Her husband, my mother's father, was foreman in a printing plant for 47 years, but he was also a marvelous athlete, playing semi-pro baseball into his fifties. Able to fix almost anything, a lover of hunting and fishing, he taught me to play chess, and became a skilled watercolorist in his retirement, and showed me that it was possible to be both manly and artistic, strong and kind.

My father's father, who'd been born an hour east of Naples, Italy, and had come to America at age thirteen, was my pal. He liked to be around me and I liked to be around him. I saw him every day of my life until his death when I was twelve. He'd pay me (as did my mother's father) to catch the horned green caterpillars that were munching on his tomato crop, and he taught me Italian card games and would play *briscola* with me by the hour, and bocce in the backyard on summer evenings. He'd started to teach me Italian a few months before he died; I'm still trying to learn.

I knew my father's mother the longest; she lived until the summer after my senior year in college. She was a wonderful cook and famously warm and kind, and she gave her children and grandchildren an example of how to be devout without being pretentious or judgmental. More than anyone I've ever known, she lived her faith, praying in every spare moment but always willing to interrupt her rosary to welcome a grandson and cook him a meal, or pour him an iced coffee and toast half a dozen slices of Italian bread. I think of her as a kind of quiet Zen master of the domestic world.

The summer she died I was doing a bit of volunteer work at the Perkins School for the Blind, my way of giving thanks for not losing my right eye in a bad stickball accident a few years earlier. I'd drive my mother's used, five-speed, yellow Mercury Capri to Watertown, walk from the school into downtown with my blind, African American friend Ernie holding my arm. We'd have a meal and talk, and then I'd walk him back to the school.

On one of those nights I was finished at Perkins and headed home—I remember blasting Springsteen's brand new album, *Born to Run*, on the tape player—when I decided to look in on my Grandmother Merullo. She had Alzheimer's by then, and was at Mass General Hospital for surgery on a facial cyst. In those years there were strict visiting hours, and I knew I was already too late, but I thought I'd go to the hospital anyway and see if I could sneak in.

I parked, walked into the building, and hustled over to an elevator the doors of which were just closing. It was filled with a couple of doctors and four or five residents, making their nightly rounds, I guess. I was an interloper, a trespasser; all the other visitors had been chased out by then. Before the elevator started up, one of the doctors said, "Where are you going?"

"I know it's after hours," I told him, "but I'm

going up to see my grandmother for a few minutes."

"Who's your grandmother."

"Eleonora Merullo."

"Go ahead then," he said. "She's a special woman."

Why he said that, how he sensed it through the haze of her late-stage Alzheimer's, I don't know, but even with most of her memory gone she seemed to have that effect on people. The loving smile was still there.

She was hooked up to machinery and when she saw me she tried to offer one of those beautiful smiles, but her face hurt too much and the smile was cut short. I leaned over and kissed her, stayed a few minutes, talking to her about things I don't remember now, then told her I loved her and headed back downstairs.

She died two days later.

Some doctors would have chased me out.

~ 15 ~

Sometimes people who have the least are the most generous.

I have a lot of stories from my six months of Peace Corps service in Micronesia. Here's one.

After a few weeks of not-very-helpful training at a luxury resort on Guam, my fellow volunteers and I were flown to the island of Truk (now Chuuk) for language and cross-cultural classes. There, after a night in a moldy hotel, we were set up, one by one, in the houses of host families. I lived in the hamlet of Koroli, in the village of Sapuk, at the far end of a rutted dirt road that stretched several miles from the capital city, Moen (now Weeno) most of the way around the mountainous island. My host parents were a couple named Samurai and Miako, who lived, along with 20 family members, in a one-story concrete house with a tin roof and an outhouse. For windows, there were square holes in the walls, covered at night with plywood.

Originally, the house had one large room, no furniture, but, in anticipation of their Peace Corps guest, Samurai and Miako had built on a small second room with louvered windows. I slept there, on a woven pandanus mat on the floor, covered by mosquito netting. The other 22 members of the household slept in sheets in the main room. Miako and Samurai received a small stipend for housing me—that was how they'd been able to pay for the construction of the small room and the purchase of the louvered windows.

I stayed there for three months. Samurai worked part-time as a driver for the local Catholic school. His son Samichi and son-in-law Antonio cut coconuts and hands of bananas and harvested the sea—turtle, eel, snail, crab, every manner of fish—to help feed the family. Miako, with the help of her beautiful daughters, Emma, Nanci, and Xenifia, cooked my meals and washed my clothes. Sometimes breakfast would be fish that had been salted and set out to dry for weeks on the metal roof. Sometimes it would be Spam—grilled or right out of the can. Sometimes we'd have just-caught tuna, barracuda, or puffer fish for the other meals, always with white rice, and usually with breadfruit, tapioca, coconut and bananas.

They drank rainwater funneled from the roof into a rusty fifty-five-gallon barrel out front, but they always 'cooked' my water, i.e., boiled it long enough to kill whatever organisms the American stomach couldn't handle.

Like about half of the twenty other volunteers, I chose to be assigned to one of the outer islands, in my case a tiny atoll in the Hall Group about sixty sea miles from Truk. (If you have a very good map of the world, look for a dot about 8 degrees north of the equator). In those days the only way to get there was the regular field trip run on the Micro Dawn. It so happened that, after our training on the big island was finished, I was scheduled, because of the Micro Dawn's itinerary, to stay several weeks longer than the other outer island volunteers.

This meant that, either I'd have to sleep on a couch in the Peace Corps office, or ask Miako and Samurai to host me after the period covered by their weekly stipend had expired.

Samurai was off at work most of the time, either driving or leaving before sunrise to climb into the jungle and gather fruit from the trees. So, when I found out the Micro Dawn's schedule, and the delay it would cause, I went to Miako and said, "I'm sorry, but the Peace Corps won't pay for me to be here anymore, and it will be weeks before the ship leaves."

Since the dialect of Trukese spoken on that island did not have the 'L' sound, people there called me Ronan or Ron, rolling the 'R' and stretching out the word so that it sounded like "Rrr-u-n."

"That doesn't matter, Rrr-u-n," Miako said. "*Esse nefinifin.* You're part of our family now. You say here as long as you want."

In fact, when it came time for me to leave on the Micro Dawn, Miako and Samurai tried to convince me to change my Peace Corps assignment to the main island, and live with them for two years—though they would not have been paid.

~ 16 ~

I started playing golf seriously when I was 45, and in the 20 years since then the game has given me so much pleasure, so many life lessons, and introduced me to so many fine people that I will always be grateful I dug out my father's old Hogan irons and hit the links again. Amanda and I and both our daughters have enjoyed many hours on the course together.

From the outside, golf looks like a foolish pastime—old, cigar-smoking men driving around in square carts, hacking up great clods of earth with metal sticks and swearing. It also has the reputation of being an entertainment of the idle rich, and calls forth images of American royalty and their tow-headed kids frolicking on the country club verandah, passing summer afternoons around the pool, traipsing along manicured fairways with caddies lugging their heavy golf bags.

Yes, some very wealthy people play golf, but I played with a good friend yesterday for $16. There aren't so many four-hour entertainments you can pursue for sixteen dollars.

And yes, it does look foolish from the outsider's perspective. As someone who played other sports in my younger days—varsity heavyweight rowing in college, hockey, baseball, karate, cross-country running, touch football and backyard basketball—I know it's not the most arduous of physical activities (though it can mean seven miles of walking up and down hills, which is, as we used to say, not nothing.)

There are legitimate environmental concerns, especially with desert courses. At the same time, I've seen a whole menagerie of birds and wild animals on golf courses around the world; and fifty or eighty acres of city land with a lot of tree growth and no apartment house sewage systems isn't the worst environmental sin I've encountered.

What's most interesting to me is the way golf illuminates character. You have to know the game well to really appreciate that, but golf is a dance of etiquette and consideration, a continual wrestling with elation and discouragement, triumph and humiliation. Even in the heat of competition, you stand still and quiet while your opponent is playing, and shake hands when the match is finished. In more casual games, you toss your friend's divot back to him to save him a few steps, or you pick up her wedge and hand it to her after she putts out.

You search for others' lost balls in the woods, wandering through the poison ivy; you offer compliments on good shots—even when your own game is in the proverbial toilet; you hold a flagstick, buy lunch in honor of a great approach shot, or slow your pace a notch to accommodate an older or less skilled player. If a stranger appears on the first tee and asks to join your threesome, you say yes without hesitation.

I've played on wonderful courses across the U.S. and, thanks to the kind editors at the late, great, *Golf World Magazine*, in Cuba, Russia, Italy, France, England, and Ireland, as well. Course etiquette is an international language, and the joys, frustrations, and challenges of the game are the same whether you're playing elegant Oakmont or the weedy local muni, at a course in New Hampshire or on one just outside Havana.

I once played with a beloved uncle who was suffering from Alzheimer's, a man who'd had me to his modest private course countless times. Though his memory and mental functioning were deteriorating, he could still swing a club, still drive the cart. On every hole, after I'd made my final putt he'd say, "What'd you make, a three?" Sometimes what I'd made was a seven, but he wanted the best for me, assumed the best, was ready with a compliment.

I have scores of golf stories, but one that comes

to mind occurred at a public course near Keene, New Hampshire, an hour or so north of my home. I'd been invited to join two older men, longtime friends, for a tournament. Bill is a two-tour, bronze-star, Vietnam combat veteran and retired lieutenant colonel. Neal is a former Catholic priest, who left the altar in protest of the exclusion of women, married a former nun, and fathered two kids.

Neal, was having a banner day, on his way to shooting a career-low round. Bill was suffering through an awful eighteen holes, one of those golf outings where nothing goes right. What I'll always remember is the way Bill held his mood on an even keel in order to keep from spoiling Neal's pleasure. I knew he was upset—knew it all too well from my own bad days on the course—but he didn't fall into a funk, didn't complain out loud, and displayed every courtesy to make sure Neal finished well.

Neal did, earning some prize money and beaming with joy. But what I remember is Bill's consideration of his longtime friend and golf partner, exactly the kind of dignified behavior the game so often reveals.

~ 17 ~

When I was a boy, the city where we lived, Revere, Massachusetts, had, in many corners, a sense of the Old World. Revere was mixed in those days— ethnically and in matters of religious faith, though not racially—and it was common to hear Italian spoken on the streets, or to ride down Shirley Avenue past stores selling kosher food, to have first-generation Irish and Polish and French and Russian and Armenian American kids in your class.

These days, that mix persists in the city, though there are many more people of color. You can walk the beach, as I did this past summer, and hear Spanish and Arabic and Russian, see women in burqas splashing in the sea, watch Central and South Americans and Africans playing soccer on the sand. In the years when my mother taught in the public schools, there were scores of Cambodian kids in her classes, their parents having fled the terrors of the Khmer Rouge.

It's never been a rich place, and there's been some tension among these different groups. But remarkably little. Native American, English, Irish, Italian, Eastern Europeans, Nova Scotians, Central Americans, refugees from the Balkan war, Africans, Syrians, Moroccans—if you want to see the real Melting Pot, swing through Greater Revere on your way to or from Boston's Logan Airport (three miles away), and walk along the Boulevard, or stop at Kelly's for clams, or Renzo's for pizza, or Rossetti's on Winthrop Beach for the special of the day, or The New Bridge in Chelsea for steak tips. And keep your eyes and ears open.

When I was a kid, the primary ethnic group was Italian American, at least in our section of the city. Some of the names on our street were Salvaggio, Ferragamo, Coppola, Imbrescia, Santosuosso, Famigletti, Siracusa and DeRosa and we had no trouble at all pronouncing them. My grandparents' yard—our yard—was something right out of the Neapolitan countryside: a bocce court, a huge vegetable garden, pear, cherry, plum, and peach trees, a grape arbor big enough to shelter family parties on a drizzly summer Sunday, a statue of Mary in a small flower garden. There was Mass in Italian at St. Anthony's, Italian bakeries, widows in black with rosaries around their wrists, (and the other side of that culture, too: the Mafiosi, the preening showoffs, the scofflaws, the street toughs, the cheats).

One of my earliest memories is from a moment

in my grandparents' back yard at 20 Essex Street. The neighbors behind that yard, people with their own grape arbor and fruit trees and an even larger vegetable garden, were Raffaelo and Teresina Losco. One day—I was three or four years old—I was out in the yard with my mother, and Mr. Losco called us over to the unpainted wooden fence that separated our property from theirs. He and my mother talked for a bit, and then he went to his cherry tree and broke off a whole four-foot branch, heavy with fruit. He came back and handed it across to me.

That gesture is symbolic of an impulsive generosity that thrived in that place and time, and is part and parcel of the southern Italian culture. Some people would have ignored the little kid in short pants holding on to his mother's leg, or given him a quick pat on the head; some might have gone to the cherry tree, picked a handful of fruit, and passed it across the fence. Not Mr. Losco. He snapped off a branch, unworried about what damage it might do to his tree, and handed the whole thing to his three-year-old neighbor. For no particular reason beyond an impulse to give.

A treasure in more ways than one.

~ 18 ~

I write this on our daughter Alexandra's 21st birthday. She has cystic fibrosis, and while she's much healthier than some people with that awful affliction, she's still had a too-large portion of suffering in her life. So here's a story of incredible generosity—in honor of her, and in honor of all the individuals and families who've been touched by the heavy hand of cystic fibrosis.

When Zanny was diagnosed in 2001, Amanda and I started doing research on the disease, and I started looking for opportunities to write about it. In the course of that research, I spoke with patients, parents, doctors, and administrators at the CF Foundation, made some lasting friends among them, and heard many stories, pieces of which would eventually find their way into my later novel, *A Little Love Story.*

One account in particular caught my attention. I pitched it to an editor at *Reader's Digest,* and she gave me the assignment to go out to San Diego and meet the people involved.

The article I ended up writing for *RD* revolved around a young man named Matthew Joyce, a charismatic guy who might accurately be de-

scribed as a Southern California surfer dude. Matt
had a particularly virulent strain of CF-related bac-
teria, and by the time he was a junior in high
school his lungs had been devastated and his
weight had dropped to 78 pounds. His only hope
for survival was a double-lobar transplant from
living donors—who had to have the same blood
type, be taller than Matt, be in excellent health . . .
and be willing to undergo a difficult surgery and
painful recovery. None of Matt's relatives met the
criteria.

A brave and generous family friend, Fred Phillips, immediately volunteered to give a lobe of his
lung to Matt. As the father of a child with CF, Fred
knew the disease all too well.

But no second donor stepped forward.

In desperation, a cousin of Matt's contacted a
local TV station, and they ran an appeal.

Dave Manglos, a law enforcement official who
worked for United States Customs, didn't know
Matt at all. Dave had been returning to San Diego
from a long, tiring assignment in Los Angeles when
he pulled over to the side of the road to take a bit
of a rest. By his account, he had some kind of ex-
ceptional moment there, a vision of sorts: he heard
a voice telling him there was something he was
supposed to do. I later spent a fair amount of time
with Dave—strong, talkative, used to some rough
encounters on the job, and not at all the kind of

guy you'd expect to hear telling you about his visions and voices.

He had no idea what it was that he was supposed to do, but the message was clear and it bothered him all the way home and for hours afterwards. That night he happened to turn on the TV news—not a habit of his—and he saw Matt's cousin's appeal. "I think I'm supposed to do that," he said to his wife.

It turned out he was a perfect match. A day before Matt would have lost his battle with CF, Dave and Fred underwent the operations in two different San Diego hospitals; the lobes were rushed to a third hospital, where Matt's surgeons had opened up his chest cavity and removed the damaged lungs. In went the new lobes. Three years later, when I saw Matt, he and his buddies were surfing at Black's Beach.

Thanks to Fred Phillips and Dave Manglos, Matt lived another seven and a half years, and got to travel the world on surfing adventures.

People with cystic fibrosis have a reputation for a) not complaining, and b) thinking of others. Matt fit that profile. In the extra years Fred and Dave had given him, he helped start Big Worm's (his surfing nickname) CF Life Foundation, which buys gifts for patients with cystic fibrosis—MP3 players, laptops, toys—to make their frequent long hospital stays more tolerable.

~ 19 ~

I had a pleasant but provincial upbringing. We did not have the money to take big, fancy trips. We lived a mile from a beachfront that was something like Coney Island, so our school and summer breaks were filled with backyard barbecues, time at the beach, sports in the street, in good years a three-day vacation in a New Hampshire motel that was owned by a friend of my father.

By the time I finished my schooling, I'd been to New York City once—for the 1965 World's Fair, to Vermont and New Hampshire, and twice to Montreal with college friends. The first real trip I ever took was with a friend nicknamed Fud (Rick Starzak) from the Brown University crew team. I'd finished my Master's year by then, Fud had just graduated. We each lived with our parents and worked for the summer, saved some money, and then, in early September, 1976, set off for California in Fud's old Ford Torino.

We headed west from Boston, stayed with Fud's uncle in Pittsfield, Massachusetts for a night, then angled northwest, up through New York state to Niagara Falls, and ended up sleeping in a field on the Canadian side of the border. West into Toronto, and then straight south through Michigan's Upper Peninsula. We didn't have any particular route in mind, though the eventual destination was Los Angeles, where Fud was determined to find acting work.

By about day two of the trip, we realized we hadn't taken nearly enough money, and so we started to look for ways to save. One of those ways included cutting back on food; another included the ancient art of mooching. My Aunt Lois had been a nurse in various parts of the country, and had friends everywhere. A travel lover herself, she was excited about my first big road adventure and had given me a couple of names of her friends, suggesting I look them up en route.

So in Lansing, Michigan, I found the phone number of one of those friends, called, and said something like, "Hi, I'm Rollie Merullo, Lois Haydock's nephew. A friend and I are driving across country, and my Aunt Lo suggested I give you a call and say hi from her."

It was such a thinly veiled plea for help that the woman—whose name I do not remember—immediately invited me and my friend to her home for dinner.

"Oh, we don't want to impose," I said, but of

course we did. We were two good-sized young men (Fud was six-four and over two hundred pounds) and eating about 75% of what we were used to eating, and we were hungry.

I quickly stopped resisting the woman's offer, she gave us directions, and we arrived at her home in time to share the evening meal with her and her husband and grown son. It was, as I remember, a large meal—meat, vegetables, potato, dessert—and Fud and I made the most of it. Over coffee, the woman asked if we needed a place to stay that night. We did. Another offer accepted. In the morning, there was a big breakfast, then a bagged lunch for the road, and then her son gave us a tour of the Michigan State Campus, and off we went.

We continued the mooching—staying with another of Fud's relatives in Chicago, and then with my mother's sister Cynthia and her family in Indianapolis, then, when we'd run out of relatives on our route, sleeping in the car in South Dakota, on a cold hillside in Wyoming, and in a cheap motel farther along in that state. At one point we were so low on cash that we had two consecutive meals that consisted of carrots and maple butter. At another point, in San Francisco, we signed up for day-laborer's work. I ended up counting nuts and bolts for a factory inventory, while Fud spent the day pouring acid from large containers into smaller ones. Minimum wage, but we were paid at the end of the workday.

We eventually made it to L.A., and stayed at Fud's brother's empty condo in Marina del Rey for two weeks—more mooching—enjoying the beaches and earning a little money for doing work for another Brown oarsman, Roger Hatheway, who had a new business there, cataloguing the preservation of historical homes. In October I hitched a ride back as far as New York with three strangers in a VW bug, borrowed bus fare from another Brown oarsman, Charlie Tansey, who was working on Wall Street, and finally made it home. Fud stayed on to pursue his acting dreams and still lives in Los Angeles, where he's made a good life for himself and his family.

As first adventures, go, it was an excellent one—some laughs, a little privation, a lot of generous souls along the route. I send out a belated thank you to everyone who fed and housed us, and especially to the woman in Michigan, who accepted a phone call from a complete stranger, and treated Fud and me like family.

~ 20 ~

I've written earlier about our country road, a two-lane tar ribbon that winds along a high valley in the western third of Massachusetts. Even though we've lived here for 30 years, I still think of myself as an urban kid, and I have an eye for the kinds of behavior I never saw growing up in the busy little city of Revere.

This is pickup country. Much of the traffic on our road comes from guys in their trucks. Once, when Amanda and I were taking a morning walk, one of them pulled to a stop near us, the driver took his rifle from the rack, jumped out, and fired across a field at a slinking coyote, cursing the beast as if he'd seen the devil. Other times I've seen country boys stop to pull a heavy fallen tree branch from the pavement, or, sometimes with my help, push a car out of a snowbank.

There are a lot of hunters, too, men in orange vests and orange caps who park their Fords or Chevies or Dodge RAMs by the side of the road and wander through the woods and fields after deer or turkey, ducks, bear, pheasant. One of them must have lost his way, because I saw him, close to dusk, step out of the woods behind our home and walk straight down our driveway to the road, shotgun over his forearm, eyes straight ahead. Not the kind of thing I'd ever witnessed, growing up in the city.

Some of these country boys race along the road, twenty m.p.h. above the speed limit. Some of them swing wide to give walkers a lot of room. Some of them might belong to the crew that tosses beer cans out the window on a late-night drive back home.

But the one I remember most is a young man I saw at the far southern end of the road, just before it meets up with the state highway there, near the center of our little town. He'd hit a deer with his big red Chevy, but instead of driving on, as a lot of people might have done, he'd stopped and gotten out. As I drove past, he was kneeling on the road behind his truck, and the deer was lying on its side there, too badly hurt to move. The man, another one of the pickup-driving country boys, was cradling the deer's head in his hands and appeared to be speaking to it.

~ 21 ~

Amanda and I are devoted travelers. When we have a little money, instead of buying a couch and side tables for the living room, or replacing a ten-year-old car with a newer model, we take a trip. Italy is a favorite destination. Over the almost 40 years of our marriage, we've spent time in Genoa and Venice and around Lake Como, Rome, Orvieto, Le Marche, Lecce, the hill towns of Tuscany and the ski villages up north. It would be hard to adequately express how lucky we feel to have been able to spend so much time in that country, to have shown it to our girls, to have traveled there with my mother and one of Amanda's sisters.

We've encountered a great deal of kindness and generosity there, eaten scores of memorable meals, and survived unscathed the death-defying antics of the Italian roadways (well, I had one small accident in Rome, years ago).

Strangely perhaps, we always avoided Naples, the city my father's parents sailed from when they came to this country in the first decade of the 20th

Century. We'd heard stories about street crime, dangerous neighborhoods, the garbage strikes and Mafiosi. We're fairly adventurous, but the idea of taking our girls into that kind of environment scared us off for decades.

And then a friend of ours, the fine painter John Recco, told us he'd spent a week in Naples with his wife and daughters, and assured us that the stories were exaggerated, that it was a place we had to see.

So two years ago, after spending a nice week in the lively Sardinian capital, Cagliari, the four of us took the overnight ferry to the City of the Sun ("You're really brave," people in Sardinia told us, when we mentioned the ferry ride). The cab driver who brought us from the port to our rented Naples apartment confirmed our worst fears. Loud and overly friendly, he proposed a handful of private excursions, didn't seem to want to take no for an answer, and, if I understood his Italian correctly, offered to purchase our older daughter's hand in marriage.

Things didn't get much better when we were shown to the sixth-floor Airbnb apartment. There were three or four locks on the door, plus a dead bolt, and when we asked the man with the keys if it was a safe neighborhood, he said, "During the day."

For the first night we hunkered down and

stayed inside, but that felt like a ridiculous thing to do on vacation. On the second day we ventured out, found a friend of John's, a hardworking 80-year-old named Vincenzo who had run a bar in a nearby neighborhood for most of his life. He gave us free coffee and pastries and, later, treated us to a walking tour of that part of the city. We went out that night and, instead of clinging to our wallets and cameras, realized that the stories were, in fact, grossly exaggerated, and we joined in with hundreds of others strolling the sidewalks, stopping in cafes and churches.

Immigrants aren't always treated well in Italy (not a stone Americans can throw), but I saw something on one of our walks that cut against that stereotype, too. A man who looked as if he'd recently arrived from Africa was pushing a heavy metal food cart along the street. It became stuck in the cobblestones. A white-haired Italian, chatting on the corner with his friends, left his conversation and helped the black man push the cart to the other side. It was a natural gesture, spontaneous, made without fuss.

Our daughter Zanny was going to stay in Naples for a few weeks after we left, and do volunteer work. When we told that to the middle-aged waiter in a restaurant called Da Carmella, a place we'd eaten at twice, the man leaned over the table and pointed a finger at our daughter. "Listen to me," he said, in a commanding tone. I thought he was going to give her a stern warning about the behavior of Neapolitan men, about the dangers of being single and female in that metropolis, but what he said was, "If you have any problem, anything at all, you come here. Understand? I don't want to know where you're staying. I don't want to know where you'll be working. But no matter what, if you need help, you come here. I don't want your father to worry, understand? And," he added, "If it's a woman problem, you come here at ten a.m. The owner will be here then and she'll help you out."

Zanny didn't have any problems in Naples. Neither did we.

~ 22 ~

During the time I was a student at Exeter—junior and senior years—I lived in a dormitory called Amen (pr. A̲-men) Hall at the southern end of campus, convenient to the gym and playing fields, and a long, cold, winter walk from classes. (Might be a metaphor there.) The school went co-ed in my senior year, and Amen is a girls' dorm now, so I can't go back to my third-floor double room and wax nostalgic, but I'm at the school frequently and often walk by Amen and think of the time I spent there, growing up.

It's a four-story brick building with white window trim, and there are faculty apartments on floors one, two, and four, so it's possible that those of us on the third floor enjoyed a bit more freedom in the years when there were lights-out checks at ten p.m. and other stringent regulations. I'm not confessing to anything, just saying it was possible.

We had a nice group of faculty in Amen in those years, though I was too shy to make much conversation with them the way some of the other boys did. The first floor apartment was occupied by Charlie and Joanie Pratt and their young son and daughter. Charlie was an English teacher, and a very fine poet, and one time he invited me and a couple of other boys who were taking a creative writing class downstairs to have tea with a visiting poet who was quite famous. I remember thinking the poet was obnoxious, rude, and full of himself, so I won't include his name here.

Charlie, or Mr. Pratt as we called him, was the opposite of that: a quiet, humble, dignified man. He'd been a hockey star at Princeton, and playing in Exeter's annual varsity-faculty game, without shoulder pads, weighing in at 150 pounds, he somehow skated circles around the guys we thought of as superstar seniors. Once in a while he'd come to a practice with the club players, too, and I have a memory of setting him up for a beautiful goal with a cross-rink pass, left wing to right.

When Joanie and Charlie retired, they bought an apple orchard not far from campus, and on one of our visits there, Amanda and I and the girls stopped in to say hi and buy a bag of Macintosh. We enjoyed a few minutes of pleasant conversation, but we had no idea that both of our girls would end up at Exeter for their last two years of high school.

By the time that happened, by the time Amanda and I were regular visitors on campus again, Charlie had passed away from brain cancer, and Joanie had sold the orchard and was living in a house near town. We bumped into her again and she offered to put us up whenever we came to visit.

Since then, we've stayed with Joanie countless times, an act of generosity on her part that has enabled us to spend much more time with our daughters than we would have if we'd had to pay for a hotel on every visit. Exeter is a six-hour round trip from home.

In her seventies now, Joanie is a human dynamo. In addition to her kindness to us (putting us up, making us meals, coming to my readings and Juliana's soccer games), she's active in every good cause within twenty miles—preparing an apartment for a poor new immigrant family, marching for racial justice, volunteering at the orchard and the food co-op, visiting ill friends, campaigning for the kinds of candidates who run on a platform of compassion and common sense, and involving herself in a dozen other charitable and civic causes. It's such a pleasure for me to have that connection to my days in Amen Hall almost fifty years ago, and an even greater pleasure to spend time with a woman who does more good in the world in one week than most of us manage in a year.

~ 23 ~

For reasons of privacy I won't name the people involved in two stories here.

The first is a woman we know who lost her husband when they were both very young, and who then raised their children on her own. For complicated reasons, this woman then ended up raising two of her grandchildren. She set her own life aside completely, never remarried, and devoted herself entirely to giving those two grandkids the kind of love and attention a mother or father should have given them, had the mother or father been capable. We bumped into one of those kids the other day. She's grown and happy, has a job, a boyfriend, and seemed, from the way she walked over to greet us at the local gas station, to have matured into a fine young woman.

The second story is similar and involves a couple we're close to but who live at some distance from us. They raised their two kids and, again for complicated reasons, ended up adopting one of their grandchildren. In this couple's case, they subsist on one modest salary, have never had enough money for a home of their own, or a new car, have never to my knowledge taken a vacation that lasted more than one night away.

They, too, have set their own lives aside and devoted themselves totally to the well being of their grandchild, and she, too, has turned into a fine young woman, playing sports, doing well in school. After a rocky early start, she's on the road to becoming a loving, capable member of society.

In both cases the 'complicated reasons' have to do with substance abuse and addiction. The damage that causes to our society is immeasurable. And so is the love and sacrifice of grandparents like those mentioned above.

~ 24 ~

Life is challenging enough if you have a face and body that looks and works like most everyone else's. For those people with what are sometimes called 'handicaps' it's much rougher.

Two such people played important roles in my life. The first, Anthony Pierni, had a cleft palate and the speaking difficulties that go along with that affliction. When I was a kid, Anthony hadn't married yet (later he would marry, and raise a family). He'd been friends with my father and members of my father's family for decades by then, since their high school years, but (along with my mother) was the only person in a very large group of relatives and family friends who'd gone to college. He was a programmer in computer's earliest days, and he seemed to sense that I was a boy who liked learning and wanted to explore the wider world.

He would come to our house on weekends and play chess with me, or give me accordion and then piano lessons. He'd take me into Boston to visit museums—an unheard of activity among the people I knew then. He'd take me to the driving range and golf course.

I don't think anyone was happier than Anthony when I finally published a novel, at age 37, after so many years of trying. I thanked him in that first book, writing, "to Anthony Pierni, for helping a young boy see the world."

Late in his life, when he was confined to a nursing home in central New Hampshire, I made the long drive north to visit him, and spent a little while at his bedside. Mentally, he was as sharp as ever, but he was in a great deal of discomfort. After an hour or so, I hugged him good-bye and as I was leaving he said the strangest thing: "I'll never forget what you did for me, Rollie."

What *I* did for *him.* !

When Alexandra, our older daughter, was diagnosed with cystic fibrosis, we took her to the Springfield, Massachusetts, CF Center every few months for breathing tests, throat cultures, and general checkups. One of the doctors there, Francis Duda, suffered from cerebral palsy and had a speech impediment and a great deal of trouble walking and controlling his limbs. How he'd made it through medical school, I don't know.

Dr. Duda exuded kindness, just what we needed to see on those visits, when we were so worried about our young girl, and had to sit there and watch a swab pushed far down the back of her throat, watch her do the breathing tests and pray the results would be good, when we had to think about the stories of people who'd died young from cystic fibrosis, or survived into early middle age, suffering terribly. Dr. Duda was famous for his jokes, often goofy jokes and puns, and he had a new one every time we went to see him. The nurses told us he volunteered to take the ER shifts on holidays, when the other docs wanted the night off.

A few days before Christmas last year I was doing some shopping in a bookstore near here and saw a beautiful young woman in her late twenties or early thirties, pushing herself around in a wheelchair, her legs shrunken and unusable. We exchanged a few words. She seemed happy and smart, had a gorgeous smile, and, well, let's say some of the other customers in the store, grumpy in the holiday rush, could have learned something from her.

"It's all what you get used to," a friend of mine likes to say. Maybe. Or maybe a portion of the people born with bodies or faces that don't look or work 'right', are given something else, some incredible determination, some amazing patience, an extra dose of the capacity to be kind, the ability to eschew bitterness and self-pity and think more about others than about themselves.

~ 25 ~

When I was single and 23, I served as one of twenty-five Russian-speaking American guides on Photography USA, the first of the three traveling cultural exchange exhibits I worked on in the USSR between 1977 and 1990. The guide's job was to stand near one of the exhibits (cameras, portrait galleries, etc.) and answer questions about America. Usually we were surrounded by a tight semicircle of visitors, two or three or four deep, asking us how much a loaf of bread cost in America (as if the price of bread were identical in all fifty states), or why we'd been in Vietnam, or why black and white people couldn't sit down at the same table in a restaurant, or why the police were always beating up students and demonstrators. The questions were a perfect reflection of the propaganda the Soviet people lived with every hour of the day in those years.

On this day, in the city of Novosibirsk in central Siberia, the crowd had moved on to another guide and I was standing there alone when a young woman came up and, after greeting me in Russian, said, "Would you want to go on a date?"

Sure, I thought, this is the classic: A pretty young blond KGB agent asking me out. But, being the slightly foolish person I was—and still am—I said, "Okay, I'll meet you at the cafe behind the ballet theater at 7:00 tonight."

I was wise enough, at least, to tell a couple of my fellow guides about the date, and ask them to report me as missing if I didn't return. During training in Washington, D.C., we'd been thoroughly briefed—in a windowless room—about the various tricks the KGB would play in order to compromise us.

But I was young, the girl was pretty and even younger, and I thought no harm would come from one meeting in a cafe. I told myself that, if I got the feeling she was trying to recruit or compromise me, I'd just take my leave, walk back to the hotel, and that would be the end of it.

Within about two minutes of sitting down with her, though, I realized there was nothing untoward going on. Tanya and I had a light meal, an enjoyable conversation, and agreed to meet again. A few more dates and we were going on 'picnics' together, each of us bringing food. We'd ride the commuter boat up the Ob River to one of the islands, we'd eat and talk and kiss, and catch the boat back to the city.

One night, we wandered around to the back side of the island and somehow missed the last return boat. Darkness had fallen. We were standing on the wooden dock, looking out across the huge river toward the lights of the city and, for different reasons, we were both in real trouble. Tanya was eighteen, living with her mother, and it would not have been a good thing for her to be out all night with a foreign boy. I had to be at work the next morning, and wasn't supposed to be out one-on-one with any Soviet, never mind all night.

After we'd stood there for a few terrible minutes, we heard the clacking of oars in oarlocks, somewhere out in the watery black night. Tanya called out to them, "Help us, please! We've missed the boat!"

And a male voice came back, "Sorry, sister. We can't take on anyone else. It's already hard to row in the current."

"Brother, please, please, please!" She called back. "My mother will be sick with worry. Please help us!"

There were two young men in the small rowboat. After another, similar exchange, they took mercy on her and rowed over to the dock. Tanya turned to me and said, "Don't say a word. They'll know you're American."

They probably knew anyway, just from my beard and Adidas running shoes, but I kept silent as we climbed into the rowboat.

The Ob is very wide at that point, hundreds of yards wide, and there was a steady current. After we'd gone only a few yards I noticed that one of the oars was a two-by-four, shaped to fit in the oarlock and the rower's hand. I could see the veins on the neck of the young man who was straining against the oars, and see, too, that he bore an eerie resemblance to Robert Kennedy.

Stroke by painful stroke, he moved us across the river. I don't know how long it took—twenty minutes, half an hour—but I kept my mouth shut. Eventually we landed on a sandy shore. The two Russian guys and Tanya and I dragged the boat up the beach. We thanked them and I walked her to the nearest bus stop. She headed home. I headed back to the hotel, where I had to spend five minutes convincing the guard at the door that I was, in fact, an American, and ought to be let in.

~ 26 ~

I had eleven uncles. Seven of them lived within a fifteen-minute walk of our house. An auto mechanic, a printer, an engineer, a professor, an employee of the phone company, a tailor, a car salesman—they visited my grandparents every week (downstairs and then next door) and I got to know all of them well.

One gave me my first car—a used, 1971 Buick—one helped me repair it. One tried very hard to teach me how to swim and took me on excursions in the marshlands between Revere and Lynn, fishing the canals there. One gave me my first job, selling hot dogs and coffee at the Revere High School football games at halftime when I was twelve years old. One, my godfather, took me out on every one of my birthdays and bought me hockey skates, or a baseball glove, or cleats, or shook my hand and passed on a ten-dollar bill to commemorate a good report card—no small gift for a kid in the 1960's. One bailed out a close friend of mine who'd borrowed money from the wrong type of person—and that uncle refused to let me pay him back. One, probably the poorest of the bunch, would flash hundred dollar bills when he'd had a lucky week, and buy all the cousins ice cream on summer Sundays.

We played bocce in the backyard and squeezed grapes into our mouths beneath the arbor, tossing away the bitter skins. We went to the same mass on Sunday mornings, and to the high school football and hockey games. I listened to them tell stories in my grandparents' kitchen or at one of our many backyard barbecues. Later, I played golf with some of them, intruding on their adult Saturday relaxation, a hacker then, slowing them down. But there was never anything but welcome.

Of the uncles who didn't live so close, and so weren't as big a part of my life, one let me ride on his farm tractor, one—shortly before he died—taught me how to twiddle my thumbs when I was four or five years old, one had a flower shop we used to visit on holidays, one lived in the Midwest and hosted Fud and me (see an earlier chapter) on our cross-country jaunt.

The uncles were, as an older cousin once said, larger than life, especially for a young boy looking around for examples of how to be a man in this world. There were troubles among them—addiction, flaws, tempers, insecurities—but there was also an incredible generosity, often from people who had little to spare. If you needed help, you called them. Sometimes you didn't have to call them. They might fix your fuel pump or your golf swing, offer a ride, a meal, a place to stay if you were traveling, tell you how to throw a punch, how to dig for clams at Revere Beach; they showed you how to look at and speak to a wife, a mother, and father, a child; one served as an expert source when I was writing a book about a gambler and needed some questions answered. One came to my baseball games, another to visit me at Exeter, a third made the long trip to drop in on Amanda and me out in the countryside.

The ones who lived close by, especially, gave me a sense of being protected in a world that could at times seem harsh and filled with trouble. Protected and loved. Every one of them is dead and gone now. I went to see them in the hospital, in rehab, sometimes hours before they died. Several of the ones I was closest to lived only into their mid-sixties. I attended their wakes and funerals.

Now I hold them all in my memory, and keep a photo of my father with his four brothers on the wall in the room where I work, a picture taken at my wedding. A proud, happy crew, in nice suits, with big smiles. They were, for me, examples of what it means to be a man who is unafraid to show his emotions—to cry, to laugh, to offer support, to demonstrate love.

Larger than life.

~ 27 ~

One block from our house in Revere was Sully's store, a one-room market with creaking wooden floors and a penny-candy case to die for. Presiding over this commercial establishment, every hour of every workday, was a man named Solomon Lefkowitz (it's entirely possible I have his name wrong; we knew him as 'Sully'). I bought something there pretty much every day, bread and milk for my mother, or a long list of bad-for-the-teeth treats for myself: Turkish Taffy, Waleecos, Mars Bars, Bolster, Butterfinger, Snickers, Three Musketeers, Sky Bar, black or red licorice, and a dozen penny candies the names of which I don't recall. In summer there was 'slush', too, usually lemon flavored, five, ten, or fifteen-cent sizes that Sully would spoon into pleated paper cups from behind the counter.

Sully was famous in our neighborhood for . . . being Jewish. That tells you a lot about the alphabet streets (Allston, Barrett, Cambridge, Dedham, Essex, Furness, etc.) neighborhood of what is now called West Revere (a real estate distinction that did not exist in the days when it was simply Revere). There was a section of "East Revere" that was completely Jewish, and there was one Jewish boy in my grade school, and another in middle school, but for the most part West Revere was a Catholic neighborhood with six RC churches in a five-square-mile city. So, for us, there was something mildly exotic about Sully.

As I remember, at least, through my little boy lens, at least, Sully was a bit on the grumpy side and seemed always to be on the lookout for someone walking out the door with a can of soup under her blouse, or a kid sneaking behind the candy case and snatching a nonpareil. I don't remember him smiling or making jokes, but the neighborhood women (his primary customers because, in those days, the men were at work) trusted him, and he was always kind to me. When I was a bit older, sixth or seventh grade, if the store wasn't busy he'd give me math problems or riddles. The one I remember was: Punctuate the following sentence: *That that is is that that is not is not.*

I took it home and worked it over in my mind for hours before presenting him with the written answer. Which proved to be incorrect. When I think about it now, that was a strange and wonderful thing for a store owner to do, take an interest in the mind of a neighborhood child.

By the time I was in high school, Sully had retired. His store has been turned into a very small house now, with a picket fence along the sidewalk and shades in the big front windows. Beside my sweet tooth, I haven't carried many memories away from my hundreds of visits to Sully's Store.

But some fifty years later I happened to put his name and place of business into one of my novels about Revere, just a passing reference. And then I happened to be signing books after a reading at the Odyssey Bookshop in South Hadley, Massachusetts, when a man approached me. He held out his hand and introduced himself as "Sully's son." We went out for coffee. Of course, Sully was frozen in my memory as a man in late middle age, and there was a certain incongruity in sitting across from his son . . . who was in late middle age.

We talked about his father, and the son—whose name I don't remember—told me that, during the lean years of the war especially, but even in the Fifties and Sixties, Sully had extended credit to the local housewives, even made small loans. Some of them were repaid, some were not; Sully, he said, didn't seem to worry about that.

~ 28 ~

My mother and dad were complicated and imperfect people. I don't want to make them out to be saints, but I saw in them hundreds of examples of grace, generosity, and dignity, and I'll try to distill those lessons down to a few paragraphs here.

My mother (the only one of seven kids to do so) finished college in 1944—Sargent School of Physical Therapy at Boston University—and immediately volunteered for military service. As an Army physical therapist, she worked at Walter Reed Hospital with men who'd lost arms and legs in the Pacific Theater, taking them out on mock 'dates' so they'd be able to function, socially, once they returned home. After she'd completed her two-year service, there and at Camp Campbell in Kentucky, she volunteered for a year in a polio clinic in Illinois, at a time when so many people were running the other way, terrified of that highly contagious disease. After serving there, she came back to Massachusetts, married my dad, set aside her career to raise three active boys, at first in a four-room apartment above her in-laws, and later in a house she and my father helped build next door. She tutored nieces and nephews in math, gave golf lessons to sisters-in-law, invited sick relatives to live with her, and nursed her parents and sisters as they aged and died.

When I decided I wanted to leave Revere public schools and go away to a private high school, she returned to the work force, as a middle-school teacher, so we could afford to pay the tuition left over after my half-scholarship. For twenty-five years she taught science to Revere boys and girls, and she worked part-time as a receptionist at the nursing home at the top of the street for another twenty-five years. In her spare time (!), she volunteered as an aide in a first-grade classroom in the same school where she herself had gone to first grade some 80 years earlier. When she turned 90, she decided that Revere's female veterans hadn't gotten enough attention, so she made an appointment with the mayor and presented the idea of a monument honoring those women, raised the funds with a bit of help from friends, researched the names of the city's 150 women vets, and presided over the placing of the stone monument that now stands on the lawn of the American Legion building on Broadway and bears all those names. It was dedicated on her 91st birthday.

My father finished high school in the depths of the Depression and couldn't afford college. He married young, lost his wife and first child in childbirth, struggled for a few years after that, then met, courted, and married my mother. A politician at heart and one-term city councilor, he worked for two Massachusetts governors, and, as their Personnel Secretaries, found jobs for countless relatives and friends, then settled into a state job connected to workers' compensation—Director of the Industrial Accident Board. In time, he grew bored with that work, and at age 50 talked his way into Suffolk Law School without an undergraduate degree. It took him almost ten years to finish law school and pass the Bar, years during which he commuted to Boston on the subway, held a full-time job he was tired of, went to law school at night, and was raising the aforementioned overactive sons.

If someone he knew was in the hospital, he visited. If the relative of a friend died, he went to the wake. If a nephew or niece needed a summer job, my father found one; if someone's kid was arrested, my father put in a word with the police chief, or the judge, or helped the family find a lawyer. Family meant everything to him. When I was fired from a job working construction in Boston in my college years, fired for no good reason, my father picked up the phone, called the foreman, and chewed him a new ear. He helped, he gave, he advised, he consoled, he bought suits at Filene's Basement for his fellow ushers at the nine o'clock mass. When he came to your pew with the collection basket, he'd tap you lightly on the chest—age four, age twenty-four—to remind you that you were loved. You couldn't leave the house without him shaking your hand and pressing five or ten or twenty bucks into your palm. He loved to laugh, loved to eat, loved his four brothers and three sisters, liked golf, and played nine holes with my mother the day before he died in his sleep, age 66.

They were imperfect, like the rest of us—my mom had social anxiety, my dad had a temper—but, like so many hardworking and generous parents, they set the bar so high for being decent human beings on this earth.

~ 29 ~

In the fall of 1977, after returning from eight months in the USSR, and some time traveling in Europe, I moved to Vermont, solo, in the hope of figuring out what I wanted to do with my life. I was twenty-four, and sailing the rough seas of a youthful confusion. I found a job making microwave sandwiches at the Killington ski area's Peak restaurant, and moved into a rooming house near the junction of Routes 4 and 7 on the northeastern edge of the city of Rutland.

The rooming house was run by an elderly couple, the Watermans, both named Fran. I had a clean, simple, second-floor room—bed, bureau, bath—and hitchhiked seventeen miles each way to the ski area. The Watermans were unusually kind people: she'd bake me muffins and cookies, and sometimes even invite me to have dinner with her and her husband. On one of my days off I accompanied the male half of the Fran duo and helped him close up their summer house on Lake Bomoseen, half an hour to the west. That errand was made a little more special by the fact that Fran had Parkinson's. He was dangerously shaky behind the wheel, but wasn't quite ready to give into that awful disease, and I think he appreciated the fact that I trusted him with my life and said nothing about his troubled driving.

Thirty hours a week I made overpriced sandwiches for skiers. I spent the rest of the time reading and thinking and walking around the town looking for both an apartment and a direction for my life. After a few weeks I rented a place on Robbins Street, in a section called The Gut. I moved out of Watermans Guest House and spent the long, frigid Vermont winter in my apartment in The Gut, found a chair, built a flimsy table, bought a mattress to put on the floor. It was a drafty place, two bedrooms and a bath with no shower, but it suited me at a time when I wasn't looking for luxury and comfort. I remember getting up at six on Saturday mornings (seven on weekdays) and walking a cold mile to my hitchhiking spot, passing the digital thermometer along the way. Some mornings it read minus 25. (Once, while still at the Watermans, I'd gone out for a walk in minus 35, just to see what it felt like. It felt cold.)

Rutlanders were exceptionally kind in those days, and might still be. I had a beard and longish hair and a bulky down jacket that made me look heftier than I am, but all kinds of people—elderly couples, mothers with young children in the car—would pull to the curb in the early morning darkness and drive me to the Mountain Road or all the way up to the base lodge. Not once was I late for work. It was the same deal on the reverse trip—skiers and locals and truck drivers stopping for a guy with his thumb out, standing on Route 4, with the sun going down and the temperature dropping like a stone tossed into a cold lake. One afternoon I stayed unusually late at work and missed the outgoing ski traffic, and was stranded on the side of the highway in single-digit darkness. After waiting there for twenty minutes, I saw a cruiser approach. A young, redheaded Vermont State Trooper was behind the wheel. He drove me to my door. Seventeen miles.

Even walking around the town on my days off I'd sometimes sense a car or pickup pulling over beside me and the driver would roll down the window and say, "Need a lift?"

The Watermans were the kindest of the kind. Just before I left Rutland, in March, I stopped in at the rooming house to say good-bye. The female Fran made me a cup of tea and sat with me for a bit, asking what I was planning to do with my life. At the end of the visit, she brought out a new book and handed it to me. *The Way of the Artist* it was called. She said, "I bought it for you because I just had a feeling it would be right." It was.

Decades later, on an assignment for *Travel and Leisure Golf,* I returned to Rutland and played Rutland Country Club. There was a snack bar at the turn, an older man behind the counter. I bought something to eat and asked if he happened to know the Watermans. He told me they'd both passed on. "The husband was mayor of the city for quite a while, did you know that?" the man asked.

Neither of the Frans had mentioned it.

~ 30 ~

Most of us have a dream—to study at a certain school, make a living doing a certain kind of work, live in a certain place, with a certain person. My dream, from the time I was twenty-five, was to make a living as a writer. It took me a long time, but I eventually reached that goal, and have enjoyed that lifestyle and that work for the past twenty years. Along the way, there were countless rejections and a hundred moments of disappointment and despair. There were lots of people—even people in the business—who told me it was impossible, or next to impossible to make a living writing novels. I remember one of my first editors telling me, "Almost nobody does that, you know, Roland," in a tone that was close to condescending.

I didn't listen. I had my dream—not to be famous, not to make a fortune from writing; just to make my living that way—and, with the help of an extremely resilient spouse, after twenty years of trying, I was able to support the family without having to work for a paycheck.

I say this to encourage, not to brag. I'm filled with gratitude, not self-congratulation. I know how lucky I am.

So many people have helped me in my writing life. This help has taken various forms: reading my work, recommending agents or magazine or book editors, encouraging me in the dark hours, lending me money, promoting my books to friends and book groups, on and on. The list is very long and if I tried to assemble all the names here I'd surely end up leaving out someone and causing bad feelings.

I will mention three people from the earliest days, before I ever published a book, and hope the others will know I won't forget their kindness and generosity.

I met Michael Miller in Williamstown, Massachusetts, in 1983, when he called and hired me to do a couple of small carpentry projects at his home on Cole Avenue. A fine poet, with five published collections now (check out *Life Lines* for one), he and I had similar upbringings, though he came of age in New York City and is twelve years older. He enlisted in the Marines instead of going to college, but is one of the most well read people I know. For years after our first conversation, he met with me every week, read and made suggestions on everything I wrote, recommended books and films, often went out with me for a pizza and beer or a game of pool and more writing conversation, and was unfailingly encouraging. When I worried because, in my thirties I hadn't yet published anything, he told me stories of famous authors who hadn't published a novel until they were 45 or 55 or 65.

Dean Crawford, whose fine first novel, *The Lay of the Land,* came out from Viking while I was still trying to get short pieces taken for carpentry magazines, also read some of my early work and made excellent suggestions. When I finally finished a draft of a novel that seemed good enough to send out, four agents rejected it without much encouragement. Dean offered to recommend me to his agent—a huge favor—and she ended up taking the book and, after more editing, selling it to Houghton Mifflin. (Dean has also written a wonderful nonfiction book called *Shark).*

I met Peter Grudin, another fine writer (*Right Here,* a novel set in southern Vermont) when I spent a year building an addition on his home in Stamford, Vermont. Not long after that complicated job was finished, I had to have back surgery. To that point, I had been writing everything longhand

and then typing it out painstakingly on Amanda's electric typewriter. Knowing I'd be laid up for weeks in our house in Pownal, and knowing how much writing meant to me, Peter unplugged his own desktop computer and brought it to our house, set it up there on the counter, showed me how to use it, and left it with me for a month. When I was able to get around a bit, he invited me to the Williams College Writing Center—he was overseeing it—and let me use the computers there, stopping by every day to help me figure out the frustrating complexities of an early Word program. I sat there for hours at a time, teaching myself to touch-type, making ten mistakes per line, and learning how to use Word. Those skills have saved me about a million hours a year since then.

I'm still friends with all three of these good men, and still grateful.

~ 31 ~

When the Soviets invaded Afghanistan in 1979, President Carter imposed various sanctions on them, including the cancellation of all cultural exchanges (and, controversially, the participation of American athletes in the 1980 Moscow Olympics.) By 1986 relations had warmed a bit and USIA's exhibit program—which I'd worked on in 1977 (see a previous chapter)—was about to be reinstated. People at the D.C. office wanted to find staffers who had some experience with the U.S.S.R. exhibits, and so a career official there, John Aldriedge, called one fall evening and asked if I'd be interested in going back. He said there was an opening for the General Services Officer job, which entailed a knowledge of physical work (I was making my living as a carpenter then) and good command of Russian. It would be a thirteen-month position, with good pay and a per diem.

I was excited at the idea of returning, in no small measure because I'd ruptured a disc, and was losing nerve function in my left leg, and could see that my carpentry days—my little business was really starting to take off—were numbered.

As mentioned in an earlier story, Amanda and I decided to take a few months off and live cheaply in Mexico, and see if the back problems would heal. It seemed the timing was good: the USSR job wasn't going to start until the following spring.

But the three months of rest didn't solve the back problems. We returned home in December of '86 and in January of '87 I had back surgery at the Pittsfield, Massachusetts, medical center. Recovery was slow and painful, but steady. The job did come through, and by the time I reported to D.C. in March, I was in pretty good shape.

The first order of duty there was to report for a physical. I was staying in Georgetown, and walked and took a subway to the USIA offices. When I arrived, the nurse handed me the usual forms. I filled them out, handed them back to her, and she glanced at them and said, "When did you have back surgery?"

"January 7th."

"Well, you might as well go home then. The government has a policy of not hiring anyone for two years after back surgery."

This was crushing news. I'd sold my pickup and emptied my bank account in order to go to Mexico. Amanda had given notice at her work at the Clark Art Institute, thinking we'd be heading to the U.S.S.R. for a year. We'd found people to rent our little house in Pownal, Vermont, and to take care of our beloved dog, Jasper. I told the nurse as much, a feeling of panic setting in. She shrugged and told me to bring it up with the doctor.

In the doctor's office, I immediately reached down and touched my toes. "See," I said. "I'm fine. I can do the job. And we've made all the arrangements, rented our house, put stuff in storage. If I can't take the job, we'll be just completely screwed."

It would have been easy—and much safer—for that doctor to read me the regulations, shake his head sadly, say how sorry he was, but he just couldn't let me take the position, not so soon after surgery. There were liability issues, regulations, he could lose his job.

But he didn't do that. "Well," he said, "I'm retiring soon, and you look okay. I'll sign off on it."

We spent thirteen months in the USSR. I drove the forklift most days, did a fair amount of heavy lifting . . .and had no trouble. I don't like to think about what might have happened if that doctor had paid more attention to the rules of the government bureaucracy and made a different decision.

~ 32 ~

I have another tale from the old days of the almost complete separation of the races in our part of the world, a story that doesn't reflect very well on me, but offered an important lesson.

In ninth and tenth grades—between Revere public schools and Exeter—I went to a Catholic school in Danvers, Massachusetts, St. John's Prep. My father would drive me to a meeting place in Revere, and a teacher who lived in East Boston would pick me up on his way to work and take me and two other boys twenty minutes north to school. On the return trip, he'd drop me off at the corner of Revere Street and American Legion Highway, and I'd either catch a bus to Broadway, or make the mile walk. There was exactly one African American boy in my class in those years, a friend of mine who'd won a scholarship from New York City and lived, with a small number of others, in St. John's only dormitory.

But my world was a white world and I'd grown up with all kinds of prejudices and assumptions that I hadn't, until that day, started to uncover.

My mother's mother was dying, and my mother would spend time at her house on Olive Street for several hours every day. Often, she'd still be there when I arrived home from a day at St. John's, so I'd go next door to my grandmother's house, sit in her kitchen, and eat whatever she put in front of me. Meatballs and *braciola*, Italian bread toasted and smothered in butter, ice coffee, milk, cookies, cake, fruit.

She was a famously warm and loving woman who'd raised eight children, all of whom lived nearby. She'd cook and clean and shop, tend to her flower garden in front of the statue of Mary, and spend her few spare hours with her rosary beads, praying at the kitchen table. Every other day, it seemed, she'd ask me if I had a 'girl'. There was always so much loving anticipation in the question, as if having a girlfriend, a love relationship, was the greatest pleasure afforded to members of the human race.

I thought she might be right about that, but the problem was, there were no girls in my school, and, even if there had been, I was far too shy, too small, too pre-pubescent to have been able to speak to them, or to have been of any interest to them.

My grandmother kept asking. The question embarrassed me, pushed me gently up against my own bashfulness and ineptitude.

Finally, one day, after countless times of having had to answer, "No, Nana, I don't have a girl." I lied and said that I did.

Her face lit up. She clasped her hands together and smiled and leaned toward me. "That's is so good!" she exclaimed. "That's the best happiness in life!"

I nodded, watched her, and then committed my sin. "But, Nana, she's a Negro."

What I expected, of course, was that she'd be shocked and disapproving. We didn't know any-one who dated or had married a "Negro"—which was the word commonly used in those days. There were, not only no examples of interracial dating or marriage on TV, there were very very few black faces on TV—in shows or commercials (though perhaps in a musical event, or in a report on a march for justice or a legal case, or a speech by Dr. King).

I expected, maybe, that she'd tell me it wasn't right, I shouldn't go around with a black girl.

But after all of one second's hesitation, Nana said, "Oh, that's-a nice. Tell me what she's like."

And I had a lesson in humility and love and open-heartedness that would last me all my life.

~ 33 ~

Parents aren't known for being objective about their kids, and I am no exception to that rule. Maybe I'm boasting here—if so, forgive me. Maybe I'm embarrassing the girls; it won't be the first time. Proud as I am of family accomplishments, the truth is, I don't take credit for the good behavior of relatives. Yes, I think Amanda and I did a good job raising Alexandra and Juliana, but I've seen lots of loving, caring parents who raised kids who turned out to be hellions, or worse, which has only solidified my belief that people come into this world with traits that belong to them alone. Parents contribute and guide, of course, but sometimes what they see in their kids has nothing at all to do with how those kids were raised, and mom and dad can just sit back and observe and admire. Or worry and mourn, as the case may be.

So, a bit about our daughters. May they forgive me.

Alexandra—Zanny—21, has cystic fibrosis, and while her particular manifestation of that horrible disease has turned out to be milder than that suffered by some people, she's still had more than her share of trouble, and she's borne it with real courage. Five sinus surgeries, scores of infections and courses of antibiotics and, even worse, three years of the mysterious fatigue illness called P.O.T.S. (postural orthostatic tachycardia syndrome) that afflicts about 1% of teenagers as they mature. P.O.T.S. took her from being an active, bright, athletic middle schooler, to someone who lay on the couch for a full year, missed all of ninth grade and part of tenth, couldn't read or sleep, was in continuous pain, and had no idea when or if she'd return to normal life.

Near the end of the P.O.T.S. ordeal, she decided she needed a change of pace and researched school years abroad. She ended up in Rimini, Italy, for a semester and came home mostly-cured and mostly fluent in Italian. Even after missing so much school, she went on, without repeating a year, to graduate from Phillips Exeter with highest honors. She decided she didn't want to go to college. She traveled a bit, came home, worked as a hostess in a beer and wings place, flew back to Europe, walked the 500-mile Camino de Santiago pilgrimage in Spain, did volunteer work in Naples, Italy, came home again to waitress, and now lives in Cambodia, where, despite ongoing health troubles, she started a foundation to help equip a school in the desperately poor provinces.

Her younger sister, Juliana, a passionate athlete from her earliest years, would often go with Amanda to the weekly volunteer music program at the local nursing home, showering both the elderly residents and the visiting preschoolers with her particular brand of warmth. Now, in her last year at Phillips Exeter, she volunteers with some of her fellow students to go and play Scrabble with elderly men and women at the Senior Center in town, and she is known for her generosity with the younger kids, helping them adjust to the arduous academic and social environment.

It will certainly embarrass her for me to tell this story but I won't mention the team she was on or the game they were playing. In one of her many soccer games, she'd scored a couple of goals and her team was safely ahead. Late in the game the ball came to her in front of the net. She was wide open for what would surely have been her third goal. Dad was on the sidelines, ready to toss his cap onto the field to mark the hat trick, but without an instant's hesitation, Juliana passed the ball back to a teammate who hadn't scored all year. It was completely reflexive and one of the more beautiful moments I've ever seen in sports.

I know every parent reading this has a list of similar moments when they were inspired by their children—their accomplishments, sacrifices, gestures of bravery or grace. Lessons that humble or inspire us.

Now I will hide and duck, because they will both come after me with a *"Dad!!!"* But the point of these stories is to highlight behavior of all kinds that has inspired me and lifted me, from all over the world, across 65 years. And it would have felt wrong to avoid mentioning two people I know pretty well, who have kept me, on a thousand occasions, optimistic about the future of humanity.

~ 34 ~

Those who have never experienced the malaise that goes under the name 'academic politics' should consider themselves fortunate. In the 1990's I had a decade or so of college teaching, and then shorter bursts—a week or ten days—of teaching in various low-residency MFA programs and writers' conferences, and I'm sad to report that I sometimes felt more at ease dealing with the low-level KGB harassment in the U.S.S.R. than with some of the more vicious maneuverings of my colleagues in pedagogy.

I don't know why that is, but I have a theory. Morally, college teaching is a dangerous profession. You spend much of your time standing up in front of eager students, mostly younger, often innocent of the world's harshest lessons. Maybe 'god' is too strong a word, but you are at least a kind of 'boss': in order to move on with their education, they have to please you by doing what you ask of them—writing assignments, reading books, coming to class prepared to discuss those books.

Except for the very occasional assessment day, there is no one looking over your shoulder. Your word is law, your style all but unimpeachable (except for student evaluations). Most of the time you know more than they do, and all of the time your job is to pass on to them what you know.

I can't think of many recipes the ego would find tastier.

But then, of course, all puffed up with your power and unquestioned authority, you occasionally have to submit to the whims of the president, or the dean, or the head of your department. The ego doesn't enjoy this, and rebels, and that rebellion can take the form of chronic griping or outright petulance.

There's something else at play, though. Your achievements as a teacher (a profession that is so often undervalued and so utterly essential to the well being of the world) are not measurable. A carpenter can gaze at his beautiful staircase and feel fulfilled; an executive can point to the bottom line successes, or a big new contract; a physician or nurse can help in a healing process that is not only visible, it's often accompanied by profuse gratitude; an athlete has his or her records and great games and applause.

Professors might have a published book or two, a prize, some notoriety within their field, but the benefits that accrue from their day to day labors can't really be photographed or measured, and there's a certain ego-frustration that can result in certain types of brainy, self-motivated, self-directed, classroom bosses.

This frustration will sometimes erupt into a pettiness and nastiness that I found shocking when I first arrived on the scene.

I won't go into detail, except to thank former colleagues like the essayist and novelist Edward Hoagland, who saved my job at Bennington (not alone, by any means, in its political turmoil) by telling me about a plot hatched—in my first semester there—by fellow teachers in my department who were determined, for their own strange reasons, to get me fired. And I'd like to salute Derek Campbell, Ron Cohen, and Carlin Romano, who stood up bravely to an authoritarian regime that first eliminated tenure and later ran roughshod over the Faculty Review Committee's recommendations.

I was the head of that committee and ended up resigning my job in protest of the firing of one of those people who stood tall. I didn't always behave perfectly myself—the moral choices and pressures were excruciating—and I understand why other faculty members couldn't take the risk those men took. Jobs were at stake, after all.

In other realms, in dictatorships, it's not jobs but lives that are at stake, and even then, even facing death or torture, some men and women exhibit a bravery that amazes me. The stakes were lower at Bennington, the offenses less grievous, but the basic response to authoritarianism followed a similar pattern: some connived and slandered; some did everything they could to avoid confrontation; those named above stood tall. They have my admiration.

~ 35 ~

If I remember correctly, there was exactly one African American family in the city of Revere in the years when I was growing up there. Everyone I knew made a point of referring to them as "good people"—partly because they *were* good people, and partly, I think, because the good white people I knew wanted to make sure it was understood that they judged others by their personal qualities, not the color of their skin.

Of course, there were Reverites who did judge people first by skin color. The N-word was commonly heard, even in jump-rope jingles. Boston was an incredibly segregated city then, with blacks in Roxbury and whites in Southie, and very few surrounding cities where there was any degree of what is now called 'diversity'.

Though we'd sometimes see an African American player on the Everett or Lynn High School football teams, or encounter a family of color on the sand at Revere Beach, it would be hard to overstate the sense we had of black people as living in a distant world, of some invisible barrier between their lives and ours.

So it was particularly remarkable that my grandfather, Giuseppe Merullo, an Italian tailor with a shop in Boston, chose to invite a black man home to Sunday dinner. I did not witness the event: it happened before I was born—in even more rigid years, which makes it, I think, even more remarkable. The man was an elevator operator in my grandfather's building, in those long-ago times when you needed a human being to tell an elevator where it should go. I'm sure my grandfather saw him every working day, and I imagine he struck up conversations, and I imagine that, in one of those conversations, prompted by the reflexive generosity we all lived with in our family, Grandpa said, "Would you come to our house in Revere for dinner on Sunday?"

I imagine, too, the trepidation the man must have felt, taking the Blue Line north from the inner city to the rough, white bastion of Revere, riding the bus a mile and a half west from the subway stop, walking the hundred yards up Essex Street, up the back stairs of my grandparents' house (no one used the front entrance), knocking on the oval door glass, and waiting to see what would happen.

What happened, from the reports I've heard, is that the meal went well, except that some of the older Old World relatives stayed in the other room, peering around the doorframe at the visitor, afraid perhaps, or impossibly curious, or perhaps, as I do, marveling at the courage of the black man, and the courage and kindness of my grandfather, both of them breaking unspoken rules.

~ 36 ~

Long time marriage is a rich and complex matter, a way to get to know a person in all her or his strengths and weaknesses. Since I work at home, and since Amanda has been a stay-at-home mom for twenty-one years, we may know each other's failings and good points even a little better than some couples approaching the forty-year mark.

We did not have kids for eighteen years—long story—but when Amanda gave birth, at age 41, she left her job as a museum photographer to stay home and raise our daughter, Alexandra. It was a decision that doubled or tripled our financial stress (and one I know many couples cannot possibly make), but neither of us has ever regretted it. A second daughter, Juliana, came along—Amanda was 45 by then and I was 48—and, while I keep pressing her to have more children (or at least keep *trying* to have more children), that was 17 years ago, and I think we will probably stop at two.

Amanda devoted herself to them completely, helping start a mom's group that went on for several years, preparing great meals, reading to them, taking them to school and meeting them after school. She taught them to swim at the Y (Dad, who grew up a mile from the Atlantic Ocean but did not really learn to swim until he was 23, thought she might be the better choice for that job), taught them to cook, to knit, to shop wisely, to manage money. She has been a steady, loving, giving mother and a fine example of a devoted wife. I've often said that, because of her consistent support, encouragement, and willingness to live an unpredictable and adventurous life and accept the financial strain that goes with it, my books should have her name on them as well, and I always thank her first on the acknowledgements page.

In her spare time (!!), she volunteered at the local nursing home, starting a program—it should be a model used nationally—where mothers (and occasionally a father or two) would bring their little ones to the nursing home for an hour every week to sing with the residents. It was something to witness: a circle of the oldest and youngest citizens singing together, the former often in wheelchairs or in various stages of dementia, the latter learning to see through the disguise of age and infirmity and feel comfortable around elderly strangers; the mothers getting a bit of a break from the solitary task of being with their toddlers and babies.

With a few missed days a year for vacations and illness, Amanda showed up at the nursing home every Tuesday, *for sixteen years.*

The girls are grown now, and both out of the house. For the past decade, Amanda has cared for her elderly mother, who lives alone in an over-fifty-five community twenty minutes away. For three of those years, Amanda was there six or seven hours a day, taking her mother to doctors' appointments, to church, nursing her through illnesses, keeping her company, shopping for her, preparing meals for her and doing various other errands. Her mother has an aide now, but even so, Amanda is often there seven days a week, sometimes for hours at a time. This week, on the day after Christmas, she met her mother at the local emergency room at 1:30 in the morning and stayed with her for two hours until she was discharged.

To illustrate another of her strengths, I might mention here some of the trials and tribulations she endures by putting up with a moody, artistic, sometimes absent-minded husband, but that part, I think, is better left to the imagination.

~ 37 ~

This is a story of bravery, generosity, and grace.

One of the members of the family I lived with on an island in the Truk Lagoon, was named Antonio. He was married to Samurai and Miako's oldest daughter, Emma, and lived in their house. Most Trukese men were short and stocky, usually five-four to five-eight, but Antonio was six feet tall, remarkably handsome, and built like an NFL cornerback. He was an exceptionally quiet man, and he and Emma both went around encased in a charismatic dignity and composure.

Since we lived in the same house, Antonio and I often greeted each other and nodded to each other, but never spoke at length. Like most Trukese men, he'd be up before dawn, climbing into the jungle to gather fruit from the trees, or going out on the ocean in a canoe or his father-in-law's precious boat, catching fish.

He must have sensed that I was bored. During

training, my language and cross-cultural lessons occupied six hours of the weekdays, but there wasn't much to do the rest of the time except snorkel and try to learn to spearfish in the waters a hundred yards downhill from our home.

One night, when the moon was full, and the sea turtles were coming into shore to lay their eggs, Antonio invited me to go turtle-hunting with him. This was a gesture of real friendship and trust, because turtles could be hunted only rarely, when the breeding season and full moon coincided, and any misstep on my part would have meant the loss of both food and the valuable shell.

Actually, as was often the case with important communications in the islands, Antonio didn't invite me directly, but passed the information on through Miako, his mother-in-law and my host mother. She asked if I'd be interested in doing something unusual; I said that I would. She said Antonio was going turtle hunting that night, and wondered if I might want to join him. I told her that I'd love to. She informed me that the plan was to meet after dinner at the stone dock the Japanese had built when they'd occupied the islands (and tormented the Trukese during World War II).

After the meal, I waited an hour or so, as instructed, then walked down the steep slick path and saw Samurai's boat tied up to the dock. Antonio was sitting in the prow. His friend, David, sat near the engine, holding the rudder. They gestured for me to take a seat on a slat in the middle.

This was serious work, feeding the family, not some fun fishing outing, and I was both honored to have been invited, and afraid of making some mistake that would mess up the hunt. David, who hadn't seemed particularly pleased to see me, started the engine and we pushed off. For a long while, we cruised quietly back and forth in the two hundred yards between shore and reef, Antonio holding a seven-foot harpoon in one hand and peering over the side. There was a coil of heavy rope between him and me, and it was connected to one end of the harpoon.

At last, Antonio spotted a turtle—a dark, round shadow eight feet below, the clear water made translucent by the moon—and made a hand signal to David. The boat sped up. We raced toward the reef, Antonio holding the harpoon over his right shoulder, his back to David and me, and using it to signal that we should follow the terrified, zigzagging turtle right or left. It was amazing to me how fast the creature could swim, how elegant its maneuvering. We came closer and closer, but then ran out of room, the turtle darting over the coral berm, and I could sense that Antonio was disappointed in David's boatmanship.

We cruised back and forth for another hour, the moon high by then, time running out. Antonio spotted another turtle—no doubt it had laid its eggs in the sandy shore and was heading to the safety of deep water. We followed this one, too, same hand signals, same fast speed, but before we reached the reef, Antonio stood over the prow and drove the harpoon with great force down into the water. The blunt end of the harpoon stayed visible above the water, wobbling slightly there. David made an immediate U-turn and Antonio went over the side.

He was out of sight there in the dark water for what seemed like a full minute, and then he surfaced for a breath, his face lit by a smile, and said the magic word, "*Pwe-pwe.*" Turtle!

I thought: *what else?* And learned only later that it could have been a sting ray. Antonio had leaped over the side into dark water and reached out a hand, knowing that he might have speared, not a sea tortoise large enough to feed the whole family for two meals, but a sting ray that could have paralyzed him with one slash of its tail.

When he surfaced again, I helped him lift the turtle—large as a Thanksgiving platter—into the boat—and then helped him climb back in. I could see the place where the harpoon's sharp point had pierced the shell. We brought it back to the dock, kept it in a small metal shed overnight, and then it was roasted in the coals for ten hours. It made for an incredibly delicious supper.

So, a week later, when Antonio asked if I wanted to go with him to his family's atoll, fifteen sea miles away, I was honored again. On a hot Saturday morning, we headed out. I'd invited two other volunteers, and Antonio had brought along his four-year-old son, Eine. For a couple of hours, we cruised across open ocean, schools of fish drawing hundreds of seabirds in front of us, flying fish coasting along beside us like creatures from another universe, before splashing back into the sea.

We spent some time with Antonio's extended family on their tiny atoll, eating fish and drinking from coconuts, and then we headed back.

Somewhere after the first hour of the return trip, the weather worsened dramatically. Strong winds whipped the ocean into whitecaps. We went through one container of gas, then another, then a third, the little boat climbing to the crests of the waves, splashing through them, and diving hard into the next trough.

My friends and I bailed, Antonio steered, Eine held tight to his father's knee.

At last, after several more hours of fighting the seas, we turned into the Truk lagoon. If anything, the waves were rougher there, the wind howling. The engine stalled. The boat turned back-end to the wind and filled with water. My friends and I frantically bailed, Eine screamed, Antonio tore at the starter cord and finally managed to re-start the engine.

In the gale, he turned to me and pointed up the coast, toward home, and then over the reef to our right, asking me what I thought he should do with his father-in-law's irreplaceable boat. I pointed over the reef. Yes, I reasoned, the boat might be wrecked, but we'd survive, at least. If we continued to fight the heavy surf, I was sure we'd sink and have to swim a hundred yards through shark-filled waters to safety.

Antonio didn't hesitate at all. He turned the boat broadside to the waves, piloted it in close to the reef, and waited there, in screaming wind and furious surf, his little son hysterical, his cargo of Peace Corps volunteers contemplating a watery grave. And then, timing it perfectly, my quiet, good friend gunned the engine and sent us flying over the jagged coral reef, the propeller clearing it by inches.

We bailed out the boat, then, walking on the uneven, unseen coral, waist-deep in surf, pushed it for another half-hour until our relatively peaceful bay and the Japanese dock came into view. Antonio's wife, Emma, was standing on the dock, completely soaked, leaning sideways in winds that must have been close to 50 miles an hour. Waiting for her husband and son to return.

~ 38 ~

The first year we were married, Amanda and I lived on Martha's Vineyard from September to June. She was teaching high school Spanish, and I was working for a carpenter. In our spare time, with a small group of year-round Vineyarders, we started a food co-op in Vineyard Haven. There was no storefront, but members could place bulk orders. One night a week we had a community dinner and showed a movie in a church basement. That attracted a small but regular crowd of people who were hoping to break up the dreariness of living through the winter there, at a time when many of the stores and most of the houses were closed and empty, and the last ferry off the island left at five p.m.

On an April night, after one of those meals, Amanda and I were driving back to our rented ranch house in Oak Bluffs in her small car. It must have been eleven o'clock. I was behind the wheel. The house was located off a two-lane road that was divided by a solid yellow line—a no-passing zone—and I slowed down and stopped to make the left hand turn.

Several cars behind us was an impatient man who had been drinking. I remember his name but will write only his initials here, JS. JS crossed the yellow line, passed a couple of cars, and came within a fraction of a second of T-boning our Dodge Colt and probably killing us both. His car rammed into the Colt's back left corner and we were thrown forward into the trees on the far side of our road. Luckily, the wheel was turned, so instead of hitting a tree head-on we only grazed it with the right front corner of the car and ended up back on the pavement, a hundred feet from our house. Amanda had been holding a gallon of milk on her lap. She squeezed it so tight that it broke and spilled all over her.

She was otherwise uninjured, or at least seemed to be. When I went back to see if anyone was hurt, I realized right away that the other driver was drunk. He was also loud and obnoxious, accusing me of not having had my blinker on. We argued briefly and then parted ways. Someone called the police. While we were waiting for them to arrive—fifteen minutes, it took—we were standing by the side of the road and I overheard a driver of one of the cars that had been behind us say to JS, "J, whatever you want me to say to the cops, I will."

When the police got there I asked them to give

JS a breathalyzer test right away. I was watching out for Amanda, who was pregnant, and after giving the police our information, we went home.

The next day Amanda and I had to go to the police station to fill out the accident report and I was worried that JS's friend had gone there and given them a made-up story. I didn't know what could have happened; maybe a fine for me for not having my blinker on, or an insurance claim we couldn't afford. We filled out the paperwork and when we stepped outside again a stranger came up to us and said, "I was behind you on that road. You had your blinker on. You didn't do anything wrong. He crossed the yellow line and passed all of us before he hit you. I just went in and told that to the cops."

We were young and naive and didn't file any kind of lawsuit, and didn't even go to court— though, a month or so later, we read in the paper that JS had been convicted of a DUI, as it was called then.

A few weeks later, Amanda lost the baby, five months into her pregnancy.

I don't think about JS very often. Sometimes I wish I'd broken his nose, or sued him, or at least gone to court and pressed charges, but I suppose we were just happy not to have been killed. And I believe that we pay for the things we do, good and bad, though I'm not sure how.

Although we didn't get his name, and in fact

never saw him again on the island, I will always remember the man who took time off from work to go to the police station that day and tell them the truth. The police might have charged JS anyway—they had the breathalyzer results—but it was still a memorable act of grace for the man to do that, in honor of the truth, if nothing else.

~ 39 ~

Amanda and I were fortunate, thanks to the school-choice law in Massachusetts, to be able to send our two daughters to the local public grade school in Williamsburg. Fortunate, in part, because, though we live in the adjoining town, the school in that town was an 18-minute drive from our home, and the Williamsburg school was six minutes away. The other part of our good fortune stemmed from the fact that there was a coterie of devoted teachers and staff at the school, women and men who'd been there for decades. Ms. Marti, Ms. Schweitzer, Mrs. Braman, Mrs. Millette, Ms. Wright, Mrs. Luce, Mrs. Korpita, Mrs. Peloquin, Ms. Childs, Ms. Black, Mrs. Harvey, Mrs. Mimicz, Mrs. Foley, Ms. Long, and Mr. O'Connor, Mr. Heffernan, Mr. O'Brien, and Mrs. Baker. And I've probably left out a few.

It's an incredibly tough job, preparing lessons for and keeping order in a classroom of fifteen or twenty or thirty young kids, an exhausting job, really, but these women and men carried it off with aplomb. Many of the parents were involved, too. The town in those days—and even now—was something out of an America from two generations ago, a small country town where people took responsibility for each other and supported the community.

Amanda and I would go to the plays, help out at field days, and attend parent-teacher conferences. Later, Amanda even ended up doing all the school photos for six grades' worth of local children. The teachers were attentive, wise, generous with their time, and we always had the sense that they and the janitorial staff were watching out for our girls (this was especially true of the no-nonsense Mrs. Lulek, probably well into her eighties by the time she retired, who watched the front door, knew every child by name, knew if they were allergic to something or having any kind of physical, emotional, or family problem, and surely would have wrestled to the ground any malevolent intruder).

This impressive cadre was presided over by a young principal named Fred Venne. Fred would go up and shovel off the roof when there was a heavy snowfall. Fred would do double-duty as a crossing guard when one of the volunteers couldn't make it. Fred liked our kids and, at one point, knowing how much we enjoyed travel, and knowing that the kids were in no danger of falling behind, advised us to take them out of school for the month of September and go to Italy. His wife was French, he told us, and they sometimes let their own kids go to France and skip a week or a few weeks of classes, believing that whatever learning they were missing out on was more than compensated for by the experience of being in another country.

When Zanny was in sixth grade and Juje in third, we took him up on that offer, and spent a month at Casa Rondini, a small family farm near Terni, in the Italian countryside. The girls found it difficult for a while when they returned, because friendships had been formed and they'd missed out on a few activities. But the difficulty passed and the memory of Casa Rondini remains, as does our appreciation for Fred Venn, Agnes Lulek, and the whole crew of teachers and custodians at the Helen E. James and Anne T. Dunphy schools.

~ 40 ~

I was at a retreat once when the retreat leader, a Tibetan Buddhist lama, put forward the idea of an earthly communal karma. Those of us who think in terms of consequences for our actions—heaven, hell, or purgatory; karma and rebirth; or simply 'what goes around comes around'—tend to think in individual terms. If I do something good or evil, then there will be positive or negative consequences for *me*. But, while not denying that notion, the retreat leader was asserting that there is also a way in which we are all partly responsible for the actions of humanity as a whole. In some ways, it's a concept that's hard to accept. Maybe climate change is an example of that—what we do or don't do has an effect beyond our individual lives; another example might be wars that are fueled, at first, by small hatreds, by words that turn into a national trend, that lead to the election of certain people, and then lead, eventually, to war and the deaths of strangers.

I don't pretend to know how it's all set up, but I

do believe our words and actions matter, and I do like the idea of consequences. If nothing else, it can encourage us to give thought to the way we behave.

Another idea I came across at a different retreat was the image of humanity as an enormous and enormously complex web. Everything we do, everything we say, touches that web and causes a ripple effect throughout creation. It's easy to see that in cases where parents bring up a child with violence, and that child grows into an adult who perpetuates the violence; or the opposite: parents who raise their kids with love and acceptance, and watch those kids turn into loving and accepting men and women.

But through a smaller lens: If you're in a foul mood and treat, say, a clerk in a donut shop unkindly, maybe that unkindness gets passed on to her family when she gets home from a tough day. And maybe that will echo through the lives of her spouse or kids, and the people they speak to the next day. . . and on and on.

I like to think of it from the positive side. I have a particular affection for the small, ordinary acts of generosity, the ones that are so fleeting as to be all but invisible. They echo and reverberate, too. Not long ago the battery on my car remote was dying, and I went to the Auto Zone in Greenfield, Massachusetts, and, not only did the man behind the counter sell me the battery, he took an extra two minutes to figure out how to open the key fob and put the battery in.

When my daughter had a car accident, a mechanic we'd never met, a man named Limpy in East Hartford, fixed the car for her—when it seemed we might have to total it—and then did more work on a return visit, for free. Just this week, an anonymous woman who worked for the Massachusetts Health Connector resolved a complicated insurance problem for Amanda, over the phone, after several frustrating letters and calls had left her in a puddle of confusion and angst.

I've been the beneficiary of so many of these acts of kindness, some of them not so small. The nurse at Berkshire Medical Center who came in and sat with me for an hour at night after I'd had back surgery and spiked a fever; Bob, the scheduler at St. Elizabeth's Hospital in Brighton, Massachusetts, who has managed, more than once, to find a convenient way for our daughters to have surgery on their school breaks; Dr. Peter Catalano, the brilliant surgeon there; the man in a bakery in Revere who refused to let me pay for a loaf of bread because it was late in the day and they were about to close; the guy in a Rome eatery who, when I told him he'd forgotten to charge me for a glass of wine, said, "It's nothing, it's a glass of wine, no problem." Cyrus, a five-year-old on a tiny atoll in the Pacific, who took my hand one day and walked along the path with me when he somehow sensed I was going through a rough patch; my friend Jerry Cohen, who took his own life after years of struggle, but was thoughtful enough, even in his suffering, to leave me his precious chisels and piles of wide-board pine; John Manley, a B.U. crew friend, who used to drive me home to Revere after we'd spent a Friday night playing pool, even though he lived in Quincy, totally the opposite direction; Rocco Trimarchi, an old North Adams carpenter, who gave me advice and, as he was retiring, sold me some of his tools at a quarter of what they were worth; Ed, a clerk in Taconic Lumber in Williamstown, cranky at first, and then a valuable source of good carpentry advice for me when I was starting out; a female friend—I know she would choose to remain unnamed—who, completely out of the blue, gave our daughter $1,000 so she could fly across the ocean and see her boyfriend because the friend knew we didn't have the money and knew my daughter had been through a rough time; our neighbor, Zevi Steinetz, who, when that same daughter was suffering from the scourge of P.O.T.S., made a three-course meal and brought it to our home; friends like Jessica Lipnack and Joyce Maynard and Craig Nova and Peggy Moss, who fed me writing work during times when I sorely needed it; Sarah Stearns, who traveled across an ocean to visit our daughter in Cambodia; Peter Sarno, who brought my backlist into print, puts together the monthly newsletter, and drives four hours out of his way to deliver my books to a bookstore; Peter Howe, the bodyworker/healer, who'd tear up my check when he knew I was having a lean year; Tim Murphy, an editor at *Golf World*, who gave me assignments no other golf editor would have risked, assignments that led me onto world-class golf courses in places like Cuba and Ireland and gave me a paycheck besides; the woman in the Naples, Italy, subway, who chased after Amanda on the platform to tell her not to carry her cell phone in her back pocket, where it would be easy prey for pickpockets; complete strangers who let you into a line of traffic, or give you directions when you're lost, or make a joke while you're waiting for the subway, or pick up a dropped glove and chase after you to return it.

There are thousands of these moments, large and small, in all our lives, gestures of solidarity, tiny sacrifices, kindnesses that will never get much attention.

It's almost as if, whatever they say they believe or don't believe, those people understand, at some deep level, that what the lama said is true: we are linked, spirit to spirit, part of one human family. Really.

Roland Merullo is an awarding-winning author of 24 books including 17 works of fiction: *Breakfast with Buddha,* a nominee for the International IMPAC Dublin Literary Award, now in its 20th printing; *The Talk-Funny Girl*, a 2012 ALEX Award Winner and named a "Must Read" by the Massachusetts Library Association and the Massachusetts Center for the Book; *Vatican Waltz* named one of the Best Books of 2013 by *Publishers Weekly*; *Lunch with Buddha* selected as one of the Best Books of 2013 by *Kirkus Reviews; Revere Beach Boulevard* named one of the "Top 100 Essential Books of New England" by the *Boston Globe*; *A Little Love Story* chosen as one of "Ten Wonderful Romance Novels" by *Good Housekeeping* and *Revere Beach Elegy* winner of the Massachusetts Book Award for nonfiction.

Merullo's essays have appeared in numerous publications including the *New York Times, Yankee Magazine, Newsweek,* the *Boston Globe,* the *Philadelphia Inquirer, Boston Magazine, Reader's Digest, Good Housekeeping*, and the *Chronicle of Higher Education.* Merullo's books have been translated into German, Spanish, Portuguese, Korean, Croatian, Chinese, Turkish, Slovenian, Bulgarian, and Czech.

He has been a frequent contributor of commentary for National Public Radio affiliates.

Some Other PFP/AJAR Contemporaries Titles

Ambassador of the Dead - Askold Melnyczuk

Big City Cat: My Life in Folk Rock - Steve Forbert

Fighting Gravity - Peggy Rambach

Girl to Girl: The Real Deal on Being A Girl Today
- Anne Driscoll

Lunch with Buddha - Roland Merullo

Make A Wish But Not For Money
- Suzanne Strempek Shea

Music In and On the Air - Lloyd Schwartz

My Ground Trilogy - Joseph Torra

The Calling - Sterling Watson

The Return - Roland Merullo

*The Winding Stream: The Carters, the Cashes and the
Course of Country Music* - Beth Harrington

*This is Paradise:
An Irish Mother's Grief, an African Village's Plight and
the Medical Clinic That Brought Fresh Hope to Both*
- Suzanne Strempek Shea

Tornado Alley - Craig Nova

Waking Slow - Ioanna Opidee

Made in the USA
Coppell, TX
23 February 2020

16100886R00085